THE RIGHT WAY TO
MAKE JAMS

THE RIGHT WAY TO
MAKE JAMS

also includes

Fruit jellies, conserves, butters, cheeses, marmalades, curds, pickles, chutneys, ketchups and fruit bottling.

By
CYRIL GRANGE F.R.H.S.

Author of
The Right Way to Grow Fresh Vegetables

PAPERFRONTS
ELLIOT RIGHT WAY BOOKS
KINGSWOOD, SURREY, U.K.

Made and printed in Great Britain by Cox & Wyman Ltd, Reading

CONTENTS

ABOUT THE AUTHOR

Cyril Grange has been a lecturer and judge to many Women's Institutes, County Federations and Food Production Societies, various County Councils and Agricultural Societies.

He is the author of six books on home food preservation, including the standard work *The Complete Book of Home Food Preservation*. He has been a B.B.C. Broadcaster.

INTRODUCTION

Our ancestors successfully made vast quantities of jams and preserves by rule of thumb to save money, provide winter food and preserve home-grown garden and wild produce.

Scientific research gave us valuable practical information which ensured safe storage, provided superior products, and avoided failures.

In recent years an awakened desire to make jams from home-grown or cheaply-bought produce has become apparent, mainly because of the high and increasing cost of commercial jams and in some instances, the poor quality.

The making of jams at home (following proved modern practice) is simple, successful, economical and money-saving and provides a delicious food, health-giving, energy-making, nutritious, appetite-boosting, useful for many culinary purposes as a sweetmeat, on bread and butter or on toast, in sandwiches, scones, and for puddings, pies, cakes and many other purposes such as fillings, sauces, icing – there is no end.

Equally valuable are preserves of jellies, conserves, butters, cheeses, marmalades, curds, pickles, chutneys, ketchups – all dealt with clearly and concisely as money-savers and health promoters.

The bottling of fruit also provides a simple and economical method to preserve home-grown produce in a manner to be able to offer it, when it is scarce, as whole fruit, mixed fruit and salad and to use it in place of fresh or canned fruits which are increasingly expensive to purchase.

The recipes given are formulated from much research and experimentation in the author's kitchen; from recipes of proved value from skilled housewives over many years and from scientific investigation by research stations at home and abroad.

1

Jars, Bottles, Covers and Equipment

The choice of jars or bottles, the type of covers and the method of covering is most important.

The paramount feature is to seal down before mould, yeasts and germs have had time to get in and then to ensure complete and safe protection with a long-lasting, airtight cover which effectively prevents evaporation, fermentation, desiccation and general deterioration while in store.

The commercial processor exhausts the jar after filling, and then fits a completely airtight screw or half-turn metal or plastic cover which keeps the product thoroughly appetizing even after fairly long store under widely varying and often unsuitable conditions.

It pays to buy the jars and fittings with screw or clip-on or half-turn caps and, after use, keep them carefully for 'next time'.

Glass Cap, Screw Band

This is a Kilner type jar from $\frac{1}{2}$ lb. upward, has a screw band and can be used for all types of processed foods including pickles and chutneys. The contents touch only glass.

Screw Cap

These follow the common commercial pattern and have a ceresin or plastic lining or ring and a metal screw cap. These can be used repeatedly so long as the metal cap shows no sign of rust or deterioration and new linings are provided.

The Half-turn Cap or Snap-down Cap

Usually of stiff plastic, it is also efficient provided it makes a complete seal when screwed or snapped down. (All types do not effect an airtight seal, so be careful to check this when buying.)

Glass Jam-jars

These are most popular and cause most trouble because the covers are either not airtight when first sealed, or they loosen slightly in store, or the actual cover material (cellophane, greaseproof paper, etc.) itself becomes slightly porous in time so as to allow air to creep in or moisture to seep out.

Honey Jars

These have metal screw caps and ceresin linings and at 4, 6 and 8 oz. sizes are excellent for 'special' jellies, butters, etc.

Covers and Seals

Covers for jams, jellies and marmalades can be the 'breathing' type which consists of a moisture and vapour-proof disc of cellulose or waxed tissue. This is the actual seal and should be the correct size to cover the surface of the jam completely, but not adhere to the sides of the jar. The outer dust cover, usually transparent cellulose, should be put on when the preserve is either hot or cold, *never* when it is tepid or luke-warm, as moist air may cool and deposit moisture on the waxed disc, and this could possibly lead to spoilage during storage.

These waxed discs and dust covers are the most popular method of sealing jams, jellies, marmalades and curds, and are generally sold in packets complete with rubber bands and labels, in both 1lb and 2lb sizes. Cling film may also be used as an outer dust cover for sugar preserves, and is best used double thickness. These covers are satisfactory in a clean, dry, cool and preferably dark storage cupboard for anything up to nine to 12 months. However, they are not wasp or mouse-proof, and excessive heat, such as storage near a radiator, will cause shrinkage in the preserve.

Most commercial jams have a sealing lid of plastic coated or lacquered metal. Somewhat similar 'twist tops' are now available for home use. These must be used with the modern jam jars which have four ridges sloping upwards on the neck. These lids do not require a wax disc on top of the preserve, and so must be applied immediately each jar is filled.

These twist tops must not be used on fruit curds

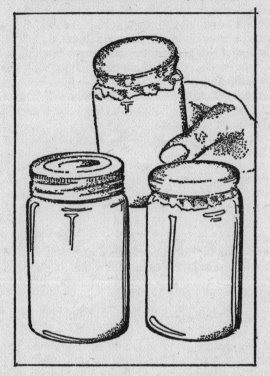

FIG. 1. Three types of covers for jam. Top – Porosan preserving skin cut to the size required, and tied with thin strong string. If the string is dampened a little before tying down the skin, it will contract as it dries, and this helps to give a really tight efficient seal. Left – a twist or screw top, which guarantees a long-lasting seal, and is the most reliable for centrally heated homes, or where storage space is near a heat source. Right – a waxed disc covered with a transparent cellulose cover.

As a final touch, before putting a batch of jam into store, wipe each jar carefully with a hot damp cloth.

containing eggs, as curds do not reach the required temperatures (curds containing eggs will curdle if boiled). Use waxed discs, and either cellulose tissue covers, or cling film. Packets of white plastic snap-on covers can also be bought, but they can only be used on the plain topped jam jars, with no ridges or screw threads.

Lakeland Plastics, Kendal, Cumbria market these, and also a comprehensive range of equipment used in all methods of preservation.

Fowler Lee of Reading also supply equipment for jamming and bottling.

Many chemists and kitchen shops also stock packets of preserving skin called 'Porosan', which can be cut to the size required. It is essential that this is tied tightly round the neck of the jar; thin strong string is best for this.

Equipment
Apart from the usual appliances found in any efficient kitchen, there are others of special value.

Balance
Able to weigh the pan plus the cooking fruit.

Bowls
Plenty, for receiving the prepared fruit and vegetable and all the water. Plastic are suitable if there is no acid, otherwise aluminium, earthenware, enamel, stainless steel or Monel metal.

Bottle Brushes
There is a special one to reach to the bottom of bottles and jars.

Bottle Tongs
Rubber-covered, spring grips for grasping the hot bottle to and from the oven or hot water.

Corer
Double ended for $\frac{5}{8}$ in. and $\frac{3}{4}$ in. cores; apples and pears.

Filling Funnel
A special, most useful necessity for filling jam, pickles, chutneys, etc. without messing the outside of the jars and bottles. Has 1¼ in. opening and 4 in. top.

Jelly Bag
Of flannel, butter muslin, cotton sheet, linen or cheese cloth, fitted to the four legs of an upturned chair. Special jelly bags can be bought of 2, 3 and 5½ quart capacity and which are used on a jelly bag stand.

Labels
All sorts, gummed or self-adhesive.

Lemon squeezer
Glass or aluminium two piece, with strainer.

Measure
2 pint graduated for ounces, spoonsful, etc., unbreakable glass.

Methylated Spirit
For testing pectin quantity of the cooking fruit.

Muslin
For making bag to hold pips, kernels, etc., during cooking.

Packing Spoon
A long-handled, small-bowled, wooden spoon for assisting close packing into jars and bottles.

Peeler
Stainless, either single or double-sided.

Jar Filler
Of heatproof glass, plastic or metal of a shape which allows for scooping up the hot jam without damage to the fingers.

Preserving Pan
Stainless steel, Monel metal, aluminium, enamel (un-cracked); not iron or zinc. Brass and copper are good for

green produce but not for those red or highly acid. For effective rapid boiling, should be wide and shallow.

Sieve

To strain first to assist speedy movement though a fine strainer. Best is of nylon.

Skimmer

Flat, perforated or slotted, wide spoon for removing stones or scum from jam, etc.

Stoner

For removing stones from cherries, peaches, apricots, plums and damsons. They can also be removed by sieving just before the sugar is added.

Spoon (*Stirring*)

Wooden preferred, and long so that you can stir without the hot jam splashing up, square or pointed end (not round), has 'stop' on handle to prevent spoon sliding down into the product.

Stone Basket

Tinned-wire, for hanging stones and kernels inside pan when cooking to extract flavour for to use as a receptacle when collecting stones from the hot jam.

Thermometer

A glass floating dairy thermometer for bottling up to 220°F.; metal-cased for 100–245°F.; sugar boiling pattern for up to 400°F. and also used in an oven. For use in water sterilizer with a hole in the lid, the pattern is 5B 18 in. and for those with a side chamber 21B.

Sterilizer

This is a receptacle in which bottles of fruit, etc., are sterilized. It must be deep enough to be able to cover the tallest bottles with the water and have a false bottom which prevents the bottles from cracking. A useful height is 12–14 in.

and it can have a hole for the thermometer or a floating 'dairy' thermometer can be used.

USEFUL HINTS

Oven temperatures (approx.)

	Electric °F.	Comparable °C.	Gas Setting
Extremely Hot	475	245	9
Very Hot	450	230	8
Hot	430	220	7
Moderately Hot	400	205	6
Moderately Warm	370	190	5
Moderate	350	180	4
Very Moderate	340	170	3
Slow	300	150	2
Cool	280	140	1
Very Slow	250	120	$\frac{1}{2}$
Very Cool	240	115	$\frac{1}{4}$

Conversion
  Fahrenheit to Centigrade: Take away 32, multiply by 5 and
    divide by 9.
  Centigrade to Fahrenheit: Multiply by 9, divide by 5 and
    add 32.

Examples:	*Fahrenheit*	*Centigrade*
	32°	0°
	65°	18°
	104°	40°
	122°	50°
	140°	60°
	158°	70°
	176°	80°
	194°	90°
	212°	100°

Capacity (approx. to nearest)

1 gill   = 5 fluid oz. = $\frac{1}{7}$ litre
4 gills = 1 pint   = 20 fluid oz. = $\frac{1}{2}$ litre
2 pints = 1 quart

	Fluid oz.	Litre
1 gill	5	$\frac{1}{7}$ (minus)
4 gills 1 pint	20	$\frac{1}{2}$ (plus)
2 pints 1 quart	40	$1\frac{1}{7}$ (minus)
4 quarts 1 gallon	160	$4\frac{1}{2}$ (plus)

$\frac{1}{4}$ litre = $\frac{1}{2}$ pint (minus)
$\frac{1}{2}$ litre = 1 pint (minus)
1 litre = $1\frac{3}{4}$ pints

Minus = rather less
Plus = rather more.

Weight (nearest useful)

oz.	grammes	grammes	lb.
1	28	500 ($\frac{1}{2}$ kilo)	1 lb (plus)
4	113	1000 (1 kilo)	2 lb (plus)
8	226		
12	340		
16 (1 lb.)	450		

Linear

Inches	Centimetres	Centimetres	Inches
1	2½		
4	10	100	40
12 (1 foot)	30		
36 (1 yard)	90		
40	100 (1 metre)		

Water Boils at 212°F. or 100°C.
Jam Sets (usually) at 220–222°F. (104–105°C.)
Jelly Sets (usually) at 220–221°F. (104–105°C.)
Fruit (etc) is Sterilized at 165–175°F. (63–80°C.)
Except cherries, pears and tomatoes 180–190°F. (82–87°C.)
Vegetables Sterilized at 10 lb. pressure (240°F.)
Syrup Sterilized at 170°F. (77°C.)

	Sugar oz.
Light syrup	4
Medium syrup	8–10
Heavy syrup to one pint	12–16

Pressures lb.	= Temperature °F.
5	227
8	233
10	240
13	245
15	250

Quick Measure
1 Wineglass   = ½ gill
1 Teacup   = ¼ pint or 1 gill = 5 fluid oz.
1 Breakfast cup = ½ pint or 2 gills = 10 fluid oz.
1 Tablespoon = 1 fluid oz.

'*Kitchen' Weights and Measures (approx.)*
Tablespoons are level not heaped and all to 1 ounce.

Fruit (Dried)	Tablespoons		Tablespoons
Currants	2	Sultanas	2
Raisins	2	Peel (cut fine)	1

Powders			
Cocoa	3	Coconut	4
Coffee (ground)	4	Coffee (vacuum)	6½
Cornflour	2	Custard	2
Flour	3	Rice	2
Rice (ground)	3	Rice (flaked)	4
Semolina	2	Sago	2½
Macaroni		Tapioca	2
(flaked)	4	Tapioca (flaked)	4
Milk (dried)	4		

Syrup			
Honey (Run)	1	Treacle	1
Sugar (most		Icing	4
sugars)	2		
Brown (soft)	3		

2

The Principles of
Successful Jam Making

What is a Jam? It is a prepared fruit cooked to a precise formula so that the natural pectin and acid are extracted and, together with added sugar, forms a colourful and tasteful mixture which sets well and keeps for a long time.

A Good Jam possesses the following qualities:

1. Firm in consistency.
2. Brilliant in colour.
3. Even in fruit distribution.
4. Soft in texture of skin and flesh.
5. True flavour of the fruit.
6. Filled to the jar top.
7. Capable of storage without the formation of syrup, crystals, mould or ferment.

A Poor Jam

1. Is runny or stiff.
2. Dull in colour, i.e. too light or too dark.
3. Uneven of texture, i.e. fruit particles at bottom as a 'layer or at top as a float.
4. As hard skin or flesh (not cooked).
5. Is lacking or masking the true flavour.
6. Is not filled to the top.
7. Deteriorates in store by becoming syrupy, forming sugar crystals, developing a mould, or by turning to wine or vinegar.

It might be useful to learn these qualities or imperfections as they illustrate in a simple form the operation of processing.

The Practical Programme

Here are the simple but needful operations:

1. Select
2. Prepare
3. Weigh and place in pan
4. Add water (if required)
5. Add acid
6. Simmer to cook
7. Test for pectin (the setting agent)
8. Add pectin
9. Add Sugar
10. Boil
11. Stir
12. Test for setting
13. Skim
14. Fill jar
15. Seal
16. Label
17. Store

OPERATION 1 – SELECT

The fruit should be *firm* and *ripe* so whatever quantity of pectin is normally present, it is not diminished through excessive ripeness.

It should be fresh so that no flavour is lost nor colour deteriorated. It should be *disease-free* (especially if purchased) in order to avoid waste and preparation time.

It should be dry, otherwise calculations may be upset by the amount of extra water within the pulp and or adhering to the skin.

If a variety is known to be low in pectin, then add 20% of that same fruit in an unripe condition. (*See* Operation 7 for pectin rule.)

OPERATION 2 – PREPARE

Soiled large fruits should be wiped over; small fruits washed briskly by running water through a cullender in which they are placed.

All decayed or squashy ripe small hard green fruits should be discarded. Selected red, white and black currants should be stalked; pears and apples peeled, cored, sliced and quartered; strawberries, raspberries and blackberries destalked when necessary; stoned fruits either left whole or stoned before or after cooking; cherry, bullace, damson, sloe, stoned; gooseberries head and tailed; rhubarb trimmed into stieks to fit the jar or cut into ¾ in. cubes.

Plums, apricots, peaches and nectarines can be peeled,

halved, the stones removed, a few cracked open and the kernels put back into the jam for flavour; but not in excess of six kernels per lb. jar or the flavour may be too pronounced.

OPERATION 3 – WEIGH AND PAN

If the method requires weight to be considered during processing, then the empty pan must be weighed at the start using a firm balance to avoid accident when the pan contains cooking fruit or jam.

By weighing, one can then deduct the pan weight later when it is necessary to calculate weight of fruit, sugar and jam during cooking.

To ensure the important speedy boiling at the finish, the depth in the pan of the fruit, water and sugar should not exceed 6 in.

To reduce the formation of sugar scum, smear over the inside of pan bottom $\frac{1}{2}$ oz. of butter or cooking margarine or pour in one teaspoonful of glycerine to each 4 lb. of fruit. The pan should be wide and shallow, excellent metals are stainless steel, Monel metal or aluminium. Enamel pans are satisfactory if there are no inside chips. Iron and zinc pans may affect flavour and colour.

Brass and copper (so often used) are good especially for greengages and green gooseberries to hold the colour, but not for red or acid fruits. Copper or iron pans are likely to destroy vitamin C in such rich fruits as rose-hips, black currants, strawberries, oranges and lemons, peaches, red or white currants, grapefruit, pineapple, tomatoes – in descending order of merit.

OPERATION 4 – ADD WATER

None, little or much is added at the beginning of the cooking for these reasons:
  (1) To extract the fruit juices;
  (2) To collapse the cell walls and release the 'jellying' pectin;
  (3) To soften skins;
  (4) To prevent scorching or burning of the fruit at the pan bottom.
  Use soft water if available.

How much water? None for juicy fruits such as raspberries red currants, elderberries, loganberries, rhubarb and strawberries; *half volume* (half as much water as there is fruit) for stiff-textured fruits such as plums, greengages and apples; *equal volume* for hard-textured fruit such as black currants (tough skin), quinces, medlars and pears; *two or three volumes* for citrus fruits such as oranges, lemons, grapefruit, and limes.

Use rather less water if the fruit is ripe or gathered wet; more water for a very shallow pan as evaporation is more rapid.

If insufficient water is added, the fruit will not be soft, the pectin will not be released, skins will remain hard and scorching may spoil flavour and colour.

If too much water is added, the juice will be weak and may need much cooking to evaporate it, with consequent loss of colour and destruction of vitamins.

OPERATION 5 – ADD ACID

For a satisfactory set, the jam must contain ample quantities of acid, pectin and sugar. If there is a lack of acid then it can easily be added.

Acidity can be roughly gauged by comparing the tartness or sourness with a mixture of one tablespoonful of fresh lemon juice (or ¼ teaspoonful of tartaric acid) dissolved in half a cup of water.

When tasted, if the fruit seems as acid as the lemon juice then no more need be added: if it is sweeter then acid will be required. Acid also brightens up the colour.

Acid Lacking Fruits

These are sweet ripe apples, unripe bananas, bilberries, blackberries (early, some acid; late, absent), cherries (cooking or sweet unripe, not Morello), figs, marrows, medlars, melons, nectarines, peaches, pears (especially ripe, dessert), pumpkins, quinces, raspberries and strawberries.

Adding Acid

There are three proved good schemes:

      (1) ¼ pint gooseberry or red currant juice, or (2) two

tablespoonsful of lemon juice, or (3) an acid solution made by dissolving one level teaspoonful of tartaric or citric acid in ½ teacup of water.

One of these is added to each 4 lb. of fruit in the pan *before cooking*, and stirred round.

OPERATION 6 – COOK

The fruit plus any water plus any acid should be brought to the boil and then the heat turned down to simmering which is slow and long (according to the fruit variety) the purpose being to, (1) cook the fruit, (2) draw out the juice, (3) soften the flesh and skin, (4) extract the pectin, (5) evaporate any excess of water (according to the recipe), (6) concentrate the fruit pulp so as to avoid the need for prolonged boiling after the sugar is added.

How Long to Cook?

The condition of the cooking fruit should be inspected frequently, Cooking will normally be sufficient when the flesh, tissues and skins are soft. Soft fruits like raspberries will take 10–15 minutes; medium stiff like plums 25–30 minutes; hard fruits like pears or tough skins like black currants 40–45 minutes.

It is *important* to simmer long *before* the sugar is added or the too early 'sugaring' will harden the skins and flesh after which no further cooking will make any improvement.

It may be necessary to simmer longer than usual if, (1) the fruit is unripe or wet, (2) the intensity of heat is low, (3) the pan is deep and carries more than a 5 in. depth.

Hot Plate

With an electric or an Esse or Aga stove which has a flat hot plate, the jam pan should also have a flat base so that the heat can be freely transferred from plate to pan.

If this is not the case then the cooking may well be slow and long. Assuming a proper pan, the electric switch should be set to low and the Aga plate to simmering.

Using a Pressure Cooker

This can be used to cook the fruit but not to make the jam after the sugar has been added.

The whistle is usually set to Notch 3. As soon as the gauge registers 10 lb., hold this for 2–10 minutes according to variety; then remove from heat, allow pressure to zero and open up.

Pressure cookers possessing no gauge have a central 3 part set of weights, or 'covers', marked 15, 10 and 5 lb. and each section can be unscrewed to disclose the particular weight marked on it.

In our case, this top 15 lb. cap is unscrewed and removed to provide 10 lb. pressure which is held as suggested above when the cooker is removed from heat to allow the pressure to drop to zero and the top half can then be removed.

The above instructions are guidelines only, it is always advisable to consult the manufacturer's book of instructions before starting on any method of preservation.

OPERATION 7 – TEST FOR PECTIN

If a jam is to set well and keep long, it MUST contain enough pectin and a simple test should be made to see if there is sufficient; and if not to add.

The fruit is cooked to the appropriate time when the test is made in this way. One teaspoonful of the clear cooked fruit juice is placed in a cold tumbler or cup and allowed to cool for 1 minute when 3 teaspoonsful of methylated spirit is poured in and shaken up. It is left for 1 minute and then poured gently out into another vessel.

If there is *ample* pectin one transparent lump will have formed; if only *sufficient*, two or four small clots will be seen which can be broken up into further blobs; if *too little* is present, the clots will be many, small and weak. Cooking should be proceeded with further in the hope of extracting more pectin or (better) to add extra pectin to the cooking fruit.

Pectin is low and required in *considerable* quantities for sweet ripe cherries, ripe figs, vegetable marrows, pears, pumpkins, ripe peaches, rhubarb and strawberries; in *moderate* amounts for sweet apples, bananas, blackberries, cooking cherries, elderberries, medlars, nectarines, peaches, raspberries and tomatoes.

OPERATION 8 – ADD PECTIN

How to Add Pectin

There are four ways by adding:

1. Home-made pectin.
2. Pectin rich fruit.
3. Lemon peel (and pith).
4. Commercially-made pectin.

1. *Home-made Fruit Juice Pectin*

From an extract of green gooseberries, red currants or green apples. Place the prepared fruit in a pan and to each 4 lb. add 1½ pints of water. Simmer until tender and strain. Next day return the pulp to the pan and add ¾ pint to each 4 lb. fruit (used at the start). Simmer for one hour, strain and then add both extracts together.

This extract can be stored in a screw-band or spring-clip covered jar and boiled (by standing jar in a pan of boiling water), for 5 minutes to sterilize and seal airtight.

In fruit deficient in pectin, add ½ pint of this extract to each 4 lb. of fruit; for fruits fairly low add ¼ pint and stir. Test for pectin and add a further quantity if the 'clot' is still weak.

2. *Pectin – Rich Fruit*

The low pectin quantity can be boosted by the addition before cooking, of fruits rich in pectin which are green apples, crab apples, bullaces, black currants, red and white currants, damsons, green gooseberries, unripe grapes, loganberries, oranges (bitter, in pith) and quinces.

Thus suitable combinations would be cherry and apples, raspberry and red currant, blackberry and apple, rhubarb and loganberry, strawberry and red currant, pumpkin and bullace, pear and gooseberry – the fruit lacking pectin being given first.

3. *Lemon Peel*

The white pith contains the pectin, so the peel should be finely sliced (and if not required in the final jam suspended in a muslin bag and removed later) and added at the rate of 4 lemons per 4 lb. fruit at the *beginning* of the cooking.

If the fruit is *also* deficient in acid, slice the peel *and* include the juice as well, e.g. for sweet cherries, ripe figs, marrows, peaches and dessert pears.

4. *Commercial Pectin*

This is bought ready either in powder or liquid form with instructions and is added after the sugar has been added and the whole brought up to rapid boiling for the time stated in the instructions. When the pan is taken from the heat the pectin is stirred into the jam and potted off.

Usually 3 lb. sugar, 2 lb. strawberries and the pectin ($\frac{1}{4}$ pint to 4 lb. of fruit or as advised) will yield 5 lb. of jam but the colour and flavour are rather different from jam made with the help of pectin from other complementary fruits.

OPERATION 9 – ADD SUGAR

It matters little whether the sugar is cane or beet or, indeed, whether it is preserving, castor, lump or granulated. Brown sugar can be used on dark fruits as it will tend to darken colour further and it also gives a distinct and not unpleasant flavour. Taking all in all, granulated sugar seems to be highly satisfactory. The cheapest is as good as the most expensive.

Hot Sugar

The sugar should be heated in an oven for these reasons: (1) to avoid lowering the temperature of the cooking fruit, (2) to return the jam to boiling quickly, (3) to evaporate any moisture which might weaken the setting, (4) to avoid possible later crystallization, especially when the acid and pectin contents are high.

The sugar should be added gradually and stirred in to dissolve but *not before* the cooking is sufficient to tenderize the fruit and extract the pectin. Then the jam should be brought up to boiling point rapidly.

If the sugar is added too soon: (1) Skins and flesh are hardened and withstand softening, (2) too little water is driven off and the jam will not keep, (3) further boiling to drive off water will destroy the pectin and setting will be prevented and (4) the jam is darkened and its flavour diminished.

The *important feature* at this junction is to simmer long and slow before the sugar is added and boil rapidly after the sugar is added.

How Much Sugar to Add?

This depends upon the quantity of pectin (as shown by the clot test), the greater the amount so the more sugar can be used to produce firm jam, of full flavour and likely to keep well.

Thus for *ample pectin* add 1½ lbs. sugar to *each 1 lb. fruit*; for *sufficient pectin* add 1 lb. sugar (a popular proportion): for *little pectin*, then only ¾ lb. sugar will be set, but the set may be weak and pectin might well have been added to make sure of a good product.

Normally a long keeping jam will contain 60% of added sugar and 5% of its own natural sugar. If it contains more, it may crystallize; if less it may ferment and go 'winey' or form mould. Five pounds of jam are normally produced from 3 lb. of sugar.

OPERATION 10 – BOIL

When all the added sugar is dissolved, heat as rapidly as possible up to 'rolling boil', that is one which continues to bubble even when it is stirred.

This is to concentrate the sugar, pectin and acid and to reach a point when on cooling the jam will make a firm set.

Boiling should continue until tests show that setting point has been reached. Further boiling will pass the setting point and will result in a sticky jam.

OPERATION 11 – STIR

The sugar is stirred into the fruit to dissolve it completely, otherwise frequent stirring is not advisable but merely to prevent any jam remaining unmoved at the bottom of the pan with a possibility of burning.

Continuous stirring usually forces bubbles down and submerges the scum and is not recommended.

OPERATION 12 – TEST FOR SETTING

Boiling is continued until the jam has reached a point when it will set and keep well and this point has to be found so that boiling can be stopped. Further boiling will turn the jam into a thick mass which will not set or will set 'solid'.

There is a choice of one of five tests: (1) Cold plate, (2) flake, (3) weight, (4) volume and (5) temperature. *N.B.*: While any tests are being made, pull the pan off the heat or boiling may progress too far.

FIG. 2. Testing setting – a spoonful of hot jam is placed on a cold plate (from the fridge), allowed to thicken for $\frac{1}{2}$ minute and then pushed with the finger nail. If (as shown) it is stiff and crinkles, then the jam can be potted.

1. *Cold Plate Test*

A small teaspoonful of the liquid part of the jam is poured on to a cold saucer or plate (which has been in the freezing part of the fridge for half an hour).

The jam will cool quickly and the edge of the jam is then pushed slightly with a teaspoon or with the finger-nail. If the surface easily wrinkles and feels stiff, then it can safely be potted off; if it still flows freely and is thin then further boiling is probably necessary.

2. *Flake Test*

A wooden spoon is dipped into the jam to collect up a liquid part, taken out, and allowed to cool quickly in a draught. The spoon is then turned slowly over to see how the jam falls off the edge.

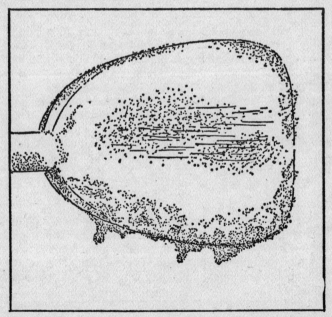

FIG. 3. This jam, in the process of boiling, runs off the wooden spoon in several thin streams and must therefore continue to be boiled until it is thicker and runs off in a single sheet or flake when it must be potted at once.

If a 'flake' is formed by the thick liquid running together and it falls off slowly and cleanly, boiling is complete; if several thin flakes run off quickly then further boiling is needed.

3. *Weight Test*

This is satisfactory for most types of jam and relies upon the fact that a good keeping jam contains 60% added sugar. Thus there is 3 lb. sugar to 2 lb. fruit in 5 lb. of jam.

The jam and spoon must be weighed at the start and allowed for in the weighing of the boiling jam at this test. The weight should be calculated by multiplying the weight of sugar added by five and dividing by three and if the jam weight is 5 lb. (or proportionally) then setting point has been reached.

4. *Volume Test*

This is a method to calculate approximately the weight of the jam from its volume, gauged by a notched stick or spoon handle. Into the empty pan is poured one 1 lb. jam-jar full of water and the water height is marked on the stick, held vertically on the pan bottom.

A further jam-jar full of water is poured in and the stick marked and so on to the top, numbering each mark.

A simple calculation (see 'weight') will tell its boiling-out weight of the properly boiled jam and this is read off on the stick, having allowed the bubbling to cease. If the level is above the mark, then boiling must continue and further tests made until satisfactory.

5. *Temperature Test*

Although precise, it may be advisable to confirm with the flake or plate test as this test only registers the percentage of sugar. Over-boiling is troublesome with some recipes.

A thermometer which goes up to 240°F. (115°C.) is needed and this is placed into the boiling jam and stirred carefully round.

If the temperature is shown as 220°F. then the sugar quantity is adequate so long as the amounts of acid and pectin were provided at the commencement.

If the flake test seems to 'disagree' it may be wise to boil on to 221° or 222°F.

OPERATION 13 – SKIM

It is wasteful to stir the scum during the boiling: better to wait until completed. Use either a wooden spoon, a plastic spatula or a perforated ladle spoon. Edge the scum to the side then scoop up and over.

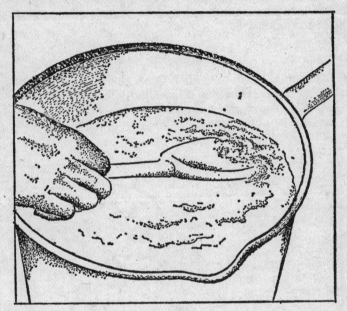

FIG. 4. Removing sugar scum from the boiling jam prior to potting.

OPERATION 14 – FILL JARS

The jars of any shape or size must be properly clean, dry and preferably hot (in an oven or on the top of a stove or in front of a fire).

As soon as the setting point is reached, draw the pan from the source of heat and fill up jars at once. To avoid soiling the jars, a special wide funnel should be used and a mug able to take at least 1 lb. jam at a time to save dripping and spilling.

It is important to fill almost to the jar rim because shrinkage after cooling will reduce the level down to $\frac{1}{4}$ or $\frac{1}{2}$ in. from the top.

When the fruit used is whole or partly so, it is well to allow some cooling (until a skin forms) before potting so that the density of the jam prevents the fruit from rising to the top. Such jams are strawberry, apple ginger, marrow, pumpkin and marmalade.

OPERATION 15 – SEAL

N.B.: Immediately each jar is filled, place on the hot jam surface a waxed circle or disc (waxed side down) so that it lays flat on the jam surface excluding air beneath it, and fits flush to the jar sides. This checks the growth of mould in store.

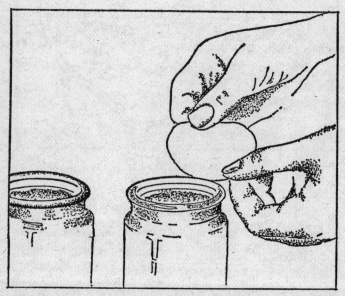

FIG. 5. Immediately the hot jam is poured almost to the top in the hot jars, it is covered with the right size waxed paper circle, the wax side downward, after which the cover is fitted airtight.

Generally the most satisfactory results are obtained by *sealing airtight immediately each very hot jar is filled*: one at a time keeping the other jars *hot*.

Special jam-jars with clip, press or screw metal or plastic caps are rather expensive but can be used again and effect a quick and definite seal.

A cheaper and good seal is that of cellulose, plastic, greaseproof or parchment sheet circle, pressed over and tied with a

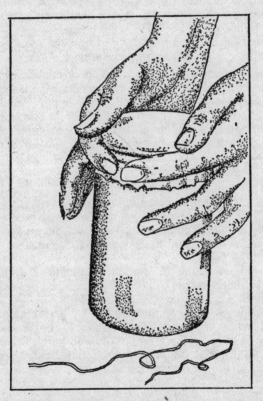

FIG. 6. A cheap and easy method of covering jam jars – two or three thicknesses of greaseproof paper each stuck together – pressed round to adhere to the jar top (as shown) and then tied tightly with thin strong string, doubled round.

double round of thin string or secured with a stout rubber band (usually stouter than are supplied).

If there is a history of mould or surface deterioration, an excellent precaution is to dip the covers or discs in surgical spirit, the surplus being shaken off before fixing.

The use of special adhesive plastic tape (Sellotape No. 1401) is successful for passing over cover joins to ensure their being airtight.

It is quite in order to use any size type of jar so long as it is thoroughly clean, sterile, undamaged and preferably of clear white glass.

OPERATION 16 – STORE

This is important and a place (room or cupboard) in the house or out-buildings should be found which is cool, frost-proof, dry, dark, airy, wasp and mouse-free. A damp place will lead to mould attacking the cover and the disc; exposure to light will spoil colour brilliancy; a warm cupboard will encourage evaporation and shrinkage; a frosty loft may split the jars.

OPERATION 17 – LABEL

Just as important! They can be home-made, cut from 10 in. ×8 in. sheets of gummed paper, professionally-made plain, bordered, white or coloured, pictured, square, oval or round and printed with name. Some plastic labels refuse to adhere until the jars are cold.

They should name the jam and date made. Helpful brief details of manufacture can be put on the labels or better in a little book, kept for the purpose.

If one is exhibiting, points are lost for untidiness and for using an unauthorized label. Old labels can usually be removed with an application of nail varnish remover, methylated spirits, white spirits or cleaning fluid.

So much for the programme of action.

TRACING MISTAKES

Mould (mildew)

Loose fitting cap; damp storage (especially with adhesive cover); sealing when warm (should be very hot) and so enclosing mould spores; sugar content below 60%; thin liquid consistency.

This jam can be boiled up after the mould has been spooned off, repotted and used for cooking purposes.

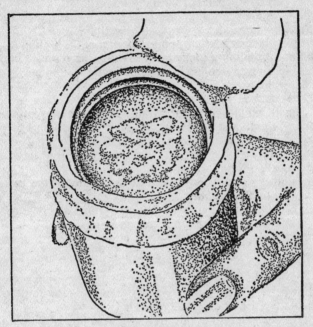

FIG. 7. An example of mould growth spreading on the top surface of the jam.

Sugar Crystals

Too long boiling and thus high sugar content; early adding of too much sugar; adding of acid after adding sugar; long cooking to make long and soft crystals of invert sugar; insufficient acid when crystals are sucrose and are hard, gritty and granulated; chemical failure of the sugar (sucrose) to be hydrolized (converted) into levulose and destrose sugar.

Poor Set

Fruit not cooked long enough to extract the natural

pectin; low pectin content of fruit which requires assistance; not sufficient water evaporated off during cooking; too ripe fruit when pectin has lost its value; boiling too long after sugar added; too much sugar added in proportion to acid and pectin: severe lack of acid.

Syrupy

Long boiling after sugar added well past the pectin setting point to result in a sticky mass of caramelized syrup; could also result from the use of overripe fruit.

Fermentation

Small bubbles are seen within the jam jars; yeasts are acting upon jam which is not set firm, pointing to an insufficient sugar content or too short simmering to cook and reduce water content: not covered airtight; warm storage.

Bubbles can also be formed at the potting if the jam is allowed to become quite tepid.

(This jam can be emptied from the jars and boiled up to increase sugar content, repotted in hot jars and used for cooking.)

Uneven Distribution

With jams where particles remain distinguishable (e.g. strawberries and marrow ginger), it is common for these pieces to rise to the top half of the jar.

They can be kept evenly arranged if the jam is allowed to cool until a skin forms upon the surface after which the jam is stirred to distribute the particles and then potted.

It is advisable to dip the wax circle and the cover in surgical spirit before fixing in order to kill mould, etc.

Shrinkage

Not filling jars up to the top; use of covers which are not airtight or leak air in warm or damp storage.

HOW TO MAKE FRUIT ACID (AND PECTIN)

It is convenient to have a supply of home-made fruit acid if only to save the cost of purchasing expensive lemons. The

Fig. 8. Straining cooked fruit by squeezing through butter muslin
to extract the juice for jelly making.

method is simple and the product also supplies the important
pectin.

Either gooseberries or red currants are simmered with an
equal volume of water for half an hour, encouraging the
production of juice by crushing down the fruits whilst
heating.

The mass is then coarsely strained through a plastic or
hair sieve or butter muslin merely to hold back the pulp, not
to produce a clear liquid.

Two and a half to 3 lb. of fruit will produce a good pint of
juice and this should be sufficient for 10–12 lb. of fruit for
jam.

This product will also contain pectin in useful amounts
(see page 26).

As the fruit acid will probably be useful at a later date, it
should be poured into small screw-band or screw-cap

FIG. 9. Pressing the fruit pulp through a hair sieve to remove the large pieces (pips, skins, stalks, etc.) for making of fruit butter, cheese or jelly.

bottles, e.g. mineral water bottles sterilized to 180°F. for 25 minutes in a saucepan of water and then screwed down quite airtight without any delay.

THE BEST SORTS OF FRUITS

If it is possible to grow or purchase and use the most suitable varieties, then the result will be superior in flavour and colour than otherwise, but where price comes into the picture, it is right and proper to jam what you can grow or obtain cheaply.
Apples Bramley's Seedling is the best all round. Lord Derby cooks down to a dull crimson. Monarch makes

good jam. Dessert varieties are not good cookers and have too little acid.

Apricots   Moorpark seems to be the only good one available. It has orange–red flesh and an excellent flavour when some of the kernels are cooked with the fruit (see page 60).

Blackberries   For cultivated sorts the Himalaya Giant ripens early and is nicely acid. The most suitable wild sorts are those which fruit early, being the most juicy and acid. Late blackberries are of little value.

Cherries   The red cooking varieties are to be recommended: Morello, May Duke and Kentish Red. On the other hand, jam any which are handy and cheap. Black cherries are colourful. Remember the need for both acid and pectin.

Currants, Black   Most sorts jam well, pride of place going to Boskoop Giant, Baldwin and Seabrooks.

Currants, Red   The best all round is Laxtons No. 1 with Raby Castle the brightest colour.

Currants, White   Although colour is missing these are useful to provide acid and pectin to other fruit of which the colour is to be retained. White Versailles is a good sort.

Damsons   An excellent jam maker; good varieties being Merryweather (true flavour), Farleigh (black) and Bradley's King (sweet).

Figs   The only one which jams well is Brown Turkey but needs both acid and pectin.

Gooseberries   Most sorts (when young green) are high in acid and pectin and useful to add to other fruits. The choice is as follows: Langley Gage, Keepsake and Howard's Lancer (all green when ripe for green jam): Lancashire Lad, Whinham's Industry super-excellent for jam, Crown Bob (all red); Careless, (another super), Whitesmith and White Lion (white when ripe), Leveller, Early Sulphur, Golden Drop (three best used for dessert, yellow).

Grapes   Any available cheap; white, red or black or ornamental.

Loganberries   Make an excellent jam full of flavour and colour – as do the hybrid brambles such as Boysenberry, Laxtonberry, Newberry and Phenomenal berry. Contain more acid and pectin than raspberries.

Mulberries   Must be fresh as they quickly go mouldy. The Black mulberry is the one to choose.

Nectarines   Only if you grow them or get them from a friend. The best all round is Lord Napier (white flesh) but for colour, River's Orange (rich orange).

Orange   Any sort according to the type of marmalade and whether solo or in mixture.

Peaches   Only if given or exchanged! Choose those with rich colour and free stone, e.g. Waterloo, Hale's Early and Peregrine.

Pears   Poor in acid and pectin. Choice is on jam quality, colour and availability; Jargonelle (musky), William's (the Bartlett for canning), Beurre Hardy (rose-water), Conference (pink flesh), Pitmaston Duchess (cooks well), Glou Morceau (delicious flavour), and Catillac (the cooking pear, amber red).

Plums   A popular jam. Any sort do well but watch progress when cooking. Here is a choice: Black Prince (damson flavour, black), Czar (purple), Oullin's Gage (golden), Pershore Yellow Egg plum and Purple Egg (suitable for good jam), Victoria (red yellow, popular), and Marjorie's Seedling (black, late). Sweet dessert sorts are not so suitable.

Quinces   Quince jelly – lovely! Rich flavour. Little acid but ample pectin. Any are good especially the Portugal for flavour.

Raspberries   These vary in flavour the choice being Lloyd George, Malling Promise, and Norfolk Giant (old but one of the best).

Rhubarb   Best for colour and flavour are Bedford Scarlet and Champagne. It does not matter much; all are good but especially those rather more mature and cheaper in summer as they set better, although they can be deficient in both acid and pectin and should be tested.

Strawberries   If you have a choice, then for flavour it is the old Royal Sovereign with the scarlet colour; if for quantity it is Cambridge 244 Favourite, a dull bluish-scarlet tinge. Huxley is too coarse and has poor flavour.

Tomatoes   Either red or yellow; medium-sized globular fruit rather than odd shaped; must be fully ripe and coloured but not too liquid inside. Has hardly any pectin.

Melon Charentais (perfumed orange), Sweetheart (salmon-pink) both cantaloupe.

Adding Flavour

It would not be sensible or practical to add chemical flavour. If the jam is made 'properly', the flavour of the fruit will be obvious and pleasant.

However some fruits are not, in themselves, possessed of a robust flavour and the general attraction of such a jam is improved by the addition of another fruit which will act as a complimentary support.

Here are some mixtures which blend well: *apple* with ginger or blackberry or date or cherry or clove or lemon or mulberry; *marrow* with ginger or pineapple, or blackberry or damson or quince; *rhubarb* with damson or black currant or raspberry or loganberry or orange; *cherry* with gooseberry or loganberry or apricot or red currant; *carrot* with almond or gooseberry or lemon; *red or white currant* with raspberry or loganberry; *cucumber* with ginger or orange; *melon* with lemon; *pear* with ginger or orange or clove or cinnamon.

Adding Colour

Although the professional processors use much flavour and colour, the chemicals are under the control of the Department of Health. It is a highly specialized branch and not to be adopted by home jam makers.

On the other hand, as with flavour, certain fruits and certain varieties of those fruits possess natural colouring which, when blended and added to a fruit which has little colour, will quite clearly improve the final preserve.

Fruits which are good for colouring are: damsons, blue and purple plums, blackberries, black currants, red currants (some sorts), mulberries and loganberries.

Fruits which lack colour and can well be improved are: pears, apples, white heart cherries, white currants, yellow raspberries, some plums, japonica, marrow and some peaches.

Sugar Saving

Sugar is costly and cannot be consumed heavily by some folk. It is interesting then to see what sort of a jam can be made with less sugar than normal. Flavour is usually especially pronounced.

It *can* be made successfully so long as:

1. There is *ample* acid and pectin (natural or commercial) in the final boiling.
2. ½–¾ lb. sugar is added to each 1 lb. of fruit.
3. Testing is done by flake or plate test (the weight or temperature test would lead to much boiling resulting in no saving in sugar for the weight of jam made).
4. Setting point – should be watched and may well be reached earlier than usual, start testing after 5 minutes hard boiling.
5. *Important*. As soon as ready, the hot jam should be poured (without delay) into hot jars and sealed *airtight* at once with stiff metal or plastic covers.

In Place of Sugar

Sugar (sucrose), an essential constitute of a jam, along with acid and pectin, ensures a good set, top flavour and long keeping. Other sweet substances have good and bad features.

Honey   This is expensive and gives much of its own flavour. It can replace ¼ of the sugar (½ at the most) but boiling time must be watched and limited or crystals will be formed. This jam has a soft set. Honey is not satisfactory for whole fruit conserves.

Treacle   Has a distinct flavour; otherwise follow the suggestions under 'Honey'.

Glucose   This is expensive, does not sweeten as much as sucrose and has no particular attribute. It may replace ¼ of the sugar but has a tendency to darken the jam. There is a risk of mould developing.

Saccharine   Its only value is its ability to sweeten. It has no value as a setting agent.

Salt   This is an economy measure and for each 1 lb. of fruit add ¼ lb. sugar into which is mixed one teaspoonful salt. Cook and boil as usual but pot hot and airtight.

It can be stiffened by adding (after the salt and sugar) ½ oz. seed pearl barley soaked overnight.

SUGAR-LESS JAM (DIABETIC)

Glycerine and Saccharine

The fruit is prepared and cooked by simmering and for each 4 lb. of fruit is stirred in 30–35 $\frac{1}{3}$rd grain (0·3 grain) saccharine tablets (dissolved in hot water) and 2$\frac{2}{3}$ pints glycerine (2 pints for 3 lb. fruit).

The mixture is then brought to boiling until it becomes thick (the setting test is not possible) when it is put hot into hot jars, preferably with a stout metal or plastic lid and sealed airtight.

Gelatine and Saccharine

Cook the fruit as usual and add: a solution of 2 oz. of powdered gelatine in $\frac{1}{2}$ pint of boiling water plus 30–35 $\frac{1}{3}$rd grain saccharine tablets (in hot water).

Bring to boil and boil for 5 minutes then pour into hot jars, put on the covers loosely, place in a water bath and sterilize by boiling for 5 minutes. Then seal airtight.

It is well to use small jars for these jams so that mould can be controlled.

PECTIN – BASE JAMS

Commercial pectins are quite safe (normally made from apples or lemons) and are valuable for getting a good set with fruits low in pectin, e.g. strawberries.

Instructions should be followed because an excess is uneconomical, wasteful and tends to mask flavour and weaken colour. However a greater weight of jam is produced because the long boiling (to extract pectin) is avoided, e.g. 2 lb. strawberries, 3 lb. sugar and pectin will yield 5 lb. jam.

A recommended method is: (1) prepare fully ripe fruit, (2) weigh fruit, add usual water and simmer till cooked, (3) add sugar (as usual) and mix well, (4) bring to rapid boiling for 2 minutes (or according to manufacturers' instructions), (5) Take pan from heat, stir in the pectin, (6) cool if advised, (7) pot and seal hot.

This improves on keeping; ideally for a month.

VEGETABLE JAMS

These jams follow the general rules for fruit jams except that they contain no acid or pectin – which must be added or the jams will neither set nor keep well.

Vegetables must be *fresh* so that flavour is at its peak; *young* and tender; *disease-free* to avoid loss and waste; *right variety* to ensure good colour and flavour.

Preparation

Carrots, cut, wash, peel, slice, cube or shred; *Marrows and Pumpkins*, wash, remove seeds and cut into cubes or strips; *Cucumber*, peel and slice thinly; *Tomatoes*, red, skinned and cut in halves; green, thinly slice. To skin dip in boiling water for $\frac{1}{2}$ minute, then into cold.

The procedure follows that of fruit, taking care to see that the acid and pectin are added either from home-made (page 27), or commercial (page 28), or by mixing in a fruit rich in these two essentials (page 27).

It may also be well to consider the addition of flavour and colours (page 43).

Varieties

These have been carefully chosen (from experimental research) to give the best results but cheap good produce should not be refused.

Carrot Autumn King (orange flesh), Chantenay (red), James' Intermediate (scarlet), Nantes (orange red).

Beet Crimson Globe (dark blood red, sweet), Long Red (black-red), Golden (orange-yellow), Snowhite (white).

Cucumber King of the Ridge (outdoor), Burpee hybrid Ridge (white flesh). These are not bitter; skin is tender and soft.

Tomato Gemini (scarlet, fleshy, sweet, few seeds); Money-maker (popular, medium sized, good quality); Golden Amateur (golden, medium-sized, thin skin).

Marrow Bush Green (dark green flesh); Bush White (creamy white); Bush Gold Nugget (orange-yellow); Trailing Delicious (bright yellow).

Pumpkin Mammoth (yellow flesh).

Gourd Sweet Dumpling.

JUDGING YOUR OWN JAMS

The ability to appraise quality in home produce goes far towards improvement in the next batch. Judging at shows and exhibitions is an interesting and worthwhile task, so here is how a judge works in this order:

1. Jar (size, style and shape) and label and sealing according to the schedule.
2. Clean and highly attractive, well filled.
3. Bright fruit colour (according to fruit variety).
4. Even distribution of fruit and absence of bubbles.
5. Open the jar and look for mould and proper fitting of wax circle.
6. Take off circle, press spoon on surface to feel any crystals.
7. Push spoon in to appreciate consistency (too soft, or too stiff).
8. Colour can be well seen by pushing a white plastic spoon or spatula down inside the sides of the jar; shown bright.
9. Spoon up some jam to note any fermentation or syrup.
10. Examine for soft texture of skins, flesh and peel.
11. Too many stone kernels included?
12. All this time, try to appreciate the aroma, fresh, pleasant and of the fruit.
13. Lastly, flavour – not too much at once – to discover true fruit flavour, satisfactory sweetness, clean to the palate, free from grittiness or juice or odd off-flavours. A mixed fruit jam should possess the flavours of each. It may be well to check up on likely faults (page 36) and jam qualities (page 21).

HERE IS A SCORE CARD

The purpose of this is to evaluate each quality and reach a total to be compared with totals of other score-carded jams and thus be able to award positions of merit.

Container
Cover, label, date   } 1
Cleanliness, wax circle

Colour   5

Quantity, texture   } 6
Quality, consistency

Flavour   8
      ─
      20

3

Successful Jam Recipes

All based on 4 lb. fruit. The average yield with 4 lb. sugar is 6⅔ lb. Follow the programme as described in Chapter 2.

APPLE

Apple Ginger

4 lb. apples, 3¾ lb. sugar, 1¼ pints water, 2 level teaspoonsful tartaric or citric acid *or* 8 tablespoonsful lemon juice plus rind and peel (in bag), 6 oz. preserved ginger (chopped fine) and 1 tablespoonful ground ginger.

Peel, core and slice apples and put under water and acid at once to stop browning. Put all in pan except the preserved ginger which goes in with the sugar. Cook, take out bag, add sugar and ginger, stir boil to setting. Yield 6½ lb.

Apple Clove

Same as above but use 10 cloves in place of ginger.

Apple and Blackberry (Bramble)

3 lb. blackberries, 1 lb. green cooking apples, 4 lb. sugar, ½ pint water.

Cook blackberries and apples slowly until soft. Add sugar, boil to setting.

A seedless blackberry is easily arranged by cooking blackberries separately with half the water until the berries are soft and passing through a coarse sieve to remove the 'pips', then adding the cooked apples into the other half of the water. Only 3 lb. sugar is necessary.

Apple and Plum

Popular and economical to use a heavy crop of each.

2 lb. of each fruit or as desired = 4 lb., 4 lb. sugar, 1 pint water.

Use cooking apples and preferably dark blue or purple plums. Peel and core apples, stone plums and weigh after this preparation to 4 lb. Cook, add sugar and boil to setting.

Apple and Raspberry

A nice wine-red mixture.

2 lb. prepared cooking apples, 2 lb. hulled raspberries, $\frac{1}{4}$ pint water.

Cook the apples to a firm pulp, add the raspberries plus the lemon pith (in a bag) and juice of 2 lemons, stir in 4 lb. sugar, boil hard and pot hot.

Apple and Black Currant

A purple 'apple' jam.

1 lb. cooking apples, 3 lb. black currants, 5 lb. sugar, $1\frac{1}{2}$ pints water.

Cook the black currants in 1 pint of water long and slow (10–20 minutes testing) so that the skins have been fully softened. Cook the prepared apples separately in $\frac{1}{2}$ pint water to a firm pulp.

Add both, and 5 lb. sugar, mix all well together, boil quickly and pot hot.

Apple and Elderberry

2 lb. apples, 2 lb. ripe elderberries, $\frac{1}{2}$ pint water, 4 lb. sugar, 2 lemons (pith, juice and grated rind).

Strip the berries from the stalk and sieve out the seeds after cooking. Simmer all together, add sugar, boil hard and pot.

APRICOT

Apricot (Fresh)

4 lb. *fresh* fruit, 4 lb. sugar, $\frac{3}{4}$ pint water, juice of 2 lemons.

Halve fruit, remove stones and add some blanched kernels (i.e. boiled in water to get the skins off them). Simmer all together (long) until tender. Add sugar, boil hard and pot.

Apricot (Dried)

Soak 4 lb. *dried* fruit in 12 pints water for 24 hours and put all into the pan with 4 tablespoonsful of lemon juice and simmer for 20 minutes. Add 12 lb. sugar, boil and pot. Half a pound of blanched shredded almonds can be put in with the sugar.

BLACKBERRY

Blackberry

4 lb. blackberries, 4 lb. sugar, ¼ pint water, 4 tablespoonsful lemon juice plus pith in bag.

Simmer the berries and the lemon juice and pith, add the sugar, boil hard and pot.

Blackberry and Apple

See Apple and Blackberry.

Blackberry and Elderberry

Both wild fruits free for the collection and blend well together.

2 lb. each berries, 4 lb. sugar, juice and pith of 3 lemons. No water.

Cook slowly, with lemons, add sugar; boil and pot.

If the combined cooked pulps are sieved, the seeds removed and 3½ lb. sugar is used the result is most flavoursome.

BLACK CURRANT

Black Currant

4 lb. currants (stripped off the stalks), 2½ pints water, and 5¾ lb. sugar.

It is important to cook long and gently for 20–30 minutes until the skins are soft and the fruit can be pressed easily between the fingers.

Then add the sugar, stir well in to mix, boil hard and pot.

Black Currant and Apple

See Apple and Black Currant.

Black Currant and Rhubarb

An economical jam to use rhubarb (sliced).

2 lb. each fruit cooked separately with 1 pint water with the currants and ½ pint water with the rhubarb.

Be sure the currants have been softened. Then mix together, add 4½ lb. sugar, boil and pot.

Black Currant and Red Currant

If one of these is short and the other makes up the weight, use the recipe as for Black currant.

CHERRY

Cherry

Choose May Dukes or Morello for red colour; black cherries for a purple colour and white-heart for a pale cream colour. All contain little acid and pectin.

4 lb. stoned cherries, 3 lb. sugar, 4 pints red currant or apple juice, juice and pith of 3 lemons.

Cook gently with the lemon and fruit juices until the halved cherries are tender, add the sugar, stir well, boil and pot.

Cherry and Gooseberry

A pleasant mixture.

3 lb. stoned cherries (white heart if you want), 1 lb. green gooseberries, (which turn red when ripe, see page 41), 4lb. sugar, ½ pint water.

Simmer all together, add sugar, boil and pot.

Cherry and Loganberry

Another excellent flavour.

2 lb. stoned cherries, 2 lb. loganberries, 3¾ lb. sugar, ½ pint water.

Simmer, add sugar, boil and pot.

Cherry and Red Currant

If red cherries used, the resultant colour is most pleasing.

2½ lb. stoned cherries, 1½ lb. red currants, 3¾ lb. sugar, ½ pint water.

Simmer all together, add sugar, boil and pot.

DAMSON

Damson
  A delicious high-flavoured jam, easy to make.
  4 lb. stoned damsons, 5 lb. sugar, 1 pint water.
  Stones can be gathered off during cooking as they come to the top. Do not overcook. Then add sugar, boil and pot.

Damson and Apple
  See Apple and Plum (page 49).

ELDERBERRY

Elderberry
  Free for the gathering and highly medicinal in value.
  4 lb. stripped ripe berries, 3½ lb. sugar, no water, juice and pith of 3 lemons.
  Simmer and sieve out seeds when fruit is soft. Add lemon, boil and pot.

Elderberry and Apple
  See Apple and Elderberry (page 50).

Elderberry and Blackberry
  See Blackberry and Elderberry (page 51).

GOOSEBERRY

Easy jam, plenty of acid and pectin.

Gooseberry
  Choose fruit colour for jam (see varieties page 41). For a green jam, choose a gooseberry of the kind that is green when ripe and use a copper or brass pan and boil rather less than normal.
  4 lb. gooseberries, 5 lb. sugar, 1¼ pints water.
  Simmer merely to soften skins, not too much. Add the sugar, boil quickly, test early for setting and pot.

Gooseberry and Cherry
    See Cherry and Gooseberry (page 52).

Gooseberry and Red Currant
    A very easy but delicious jam.
    2 lb. gooseberries, 2 lb. red currants, 4 lb. sugar, ¾ pint water.
    Simmer all together to soften skins; add sugar, boil and pot.

Gooseberry and Strawberry
    Useful to get a good set.
    2 lb. gooseberries, red when ripe if possible, 2 lb. strawberries, 4 lb. sugar, ¾ pint water.
    Cook separately and not over much. Add sugar, boil and pot.

Gooseberry and Rhubarb
    A good setter and cheap.
    2 lb. gooseberries (red when ripe), 2 lb. rhubarb (can be mature but best of a red variety), 4 lb. sugar, no water.
    Simmer all, add sugar, boil and pot.

GREENGAGE

Greengage
    Listed separately from the plums because the flavour and colour are usually superior. The most flavoursome and colourful gages are Oullins (orange), Denniston's Superb (golden), Old Greengage (green), and Bryanston (deep orange).
    4 lb. gages (stoned), 4 lb. sugar, ¾ pint water if firm, ½ pint if ripe.
    Stones can be cracked and a few kernels included at finish of boiling.
    Use brass or copper pan to assist maintenance of green colour and do not over cook.

Greengage and Apple
    See Apple and Plum (page 49).

LOGANBERRY

Loganberry
A good setter with unique sharp flavour.
4 lb. sugar, 4 lb. loganberries and as a help with some over ripe add 1 tablespoonful lemon juice.
No water. Cook slowly until soft. Sieve out seeds if desired. Add the sugar, boil quickly, test in time and pot.

Loganberry and Cherry
See Cherry and Loganberry (page 52).

Loganberry and Raspberry
Loganberry helps the raspberry to set and the delicious aroma and flavour of both are pronounced.
2 lb. loganberries, 2 lb. raspberries, 4 lb. sugar, no water.
Cook slowly together until soft, not pappy. When pips are sieved out, it improves the final jam. Add sugar, boil and pot.

Loganberry and Red Currant
A 'super' setting jam with a sharp flavour.
2 lb. loganberries, 2 lb. red currants, 4 lb. sugar, $\frac{1}{2}$ pint water for the currants which cook separately. Then mix together, stir well, add sugar, boil and pot.

MEDLAR

Medlar
A unique flavour well appreciated; little acid or pectin.
Cook until tender, 4 lb. and 2$\frac{1}{2}$ lb. water, sieve and remove husks.
To each 4 lb. sieved pulp, add 3$\frac{1}{2}$ lb. sugar and juice and pith of 4 lemons. Boil and pot.

PEACH

Peach
You may have an outdoor tree which bears prodigiously!
Remove stones, crack some for the kernels.

4 lb. peaches, 3¾ lb. sugar, ¾ pint water, juice and pith of 4 lemons.

Do not over cook. It is nice to see the shape of the fruit. Then add sugar, boil and pot.

Peach and Pear
A useful combination.

2 lb. stoned and cubed peaches, 2 lb. ripe but firm pears cut into cubes, 4 lb. sugar, ¾ pint water, juice and pith of 4 lemons.

Simmer all together but do not over cook. Add sugar, boil and pot.

PEAR

Pear
Little acid or pectin.

4 lb. cooking pears, 3¾ lb. sugar, juice and pith of 4 lemons, 1 pint water.

Stew the pears until tender with the lemon; may take 30–40 minutes. Place in pan, add sugar, boil and pot.

Pear jam by itself has no pronounced flavour but a choice can be made by adding the sugar and before boiling:

1 oz. root ginger cut fine or 1 dessertspoonful ground ginger: or the grated rind of 4 oranges or 1 lb. pineapple (tinned) and cut fine ½ in. or 1 lb. clean stoned dates cut fine (¼ in.)

If dessert pears are used adopt the same procedures but only ½ pint water will be required and cooking will be much reduced.

Pear and Marrow
See Marrow and Pear (page 62).

PLUM

Plum
An easy jam, quick to set and if not over boiled has a most delicious flavour (see varieties page 42).

4 lb. plums (stones removed and a few kernels put back), 4 lb. sugar, 1 pint water (½ pint if very ripe).

Simmer plums to cook but not to a mushy pulp merely to soften the skins. Add sugar, boil and pot. Over-boiling will spoil flavour and colour.

Plum and Apple

See Apple and Plum (page 49).

Plum and Elderberry

A pleasing combination of flavours.

3 lb. stoned plums, 1 lb. elderberries (or can be half and half), ½ pint water, 4 lb. sugar.

Cook each separately, add together, add sugar, boil and pot.

QUINCE

Quince

This can possess the most attractive and unique flavour of all. Short of acid, ample pectin.

4 lb. quinces, peel and core and either cut into cubes or globes or grate coarsely; juice of 2 lemons, 5½ lb. sugar, 3–4 pints water according to ripeness.

Simmer slowly until tender (20–35 minutes), add lemon juice and sugar, boil and pot.

Quince and Apple

Only if you want to eke out the quinces!

2 lb. prepared quinces, 2 lb. prepared cooking apples, 4¼ lb. sugar, 2 pints water.

Cook separately as apples will not take so long. Add together, add sugar, boil and pot.

RASPBERRY

Raspberry

Not an easy jam, no acid or pectin, inclined to be thin. But delicious aroma and flavour (see varieties page 42).

Recipe 1

4 lb. raspberries, 3¼ lb. sugar, no water.

Simmer to extract juice, then add sugar, boil very quickly, set is not strong but do not be late in potting and seal airtight.

Recipe 2

A more certain plan is to add acid and pectin like this:
4 lb. raspberries, juice and pith of 3 lemons, 4½ lb. sugar, no water. (The pith should be in a muslin bag and removed after cooking.)

Simmer gently with the lemon until medium soft (15–18 minutes), add sugar, boil quickly for 3–3½ minutes, pot and seal airtight.

(Home-made fruit pectin can also be used successfully (page 27) especially to make *Seedless Raspberry* by sieving out the pips before adding the sugar).

Raspberry and Apple

See Apple and Raspberry (page 50).

Raspberry and Loganberry

See Loganberry and Raspberry (page 55).

Raspberry and Red Currant

An easy, foolproof, delicious jam, easy to set.
2 lb. raspberries, 2 lb. red currants, ½ pint water, 4¼ lb. sugar.

Cook red currants separately, add raspberries, simmer, add sugar, boil and pot.

Raspberry and Strawberry

Equal weight of each fruit, then follow as raspberry recipe 2 (page 57).

RED CURRANT

Red Currant

4 lb. currants, ½ pint water, 4½–5 lb. sugar.
Cook the currants gently to extract the juice, pass through

sieve to collect up the many seeds, return pulp to pan, add the sugar, boil and pot.

White currants are best made into jelly or added to red or black currants. Currants are a rich source of pectin (see page 27).

RHUBARB

Rhubarb

A cheap economical jam with rhubarb usually in the garden. No acid or pectin.

4 lb. rhubarb peeled or cut into $\frac{1}{2}$ in. pieces, 4 lb. sugar, pith and juice of 2 lemons, no water. (The pith should be in a muslin bag and removed after cooking).

A good set and complementary flavour is got with the adding of pectin in form of apple, currant or gooseberry juice (page 27). Cook rhubarb soft (not mushy), add lemon, boil and pot.

Rhubarb and Ginger

As above plus 2 dessertspoonsful ground ginger added during cooking.

Rhubarb and Black Currant

See Black Currant and Rhubarb (page 52).

Rhubarb and Gooseberry

See Gooseberry and Rhubarb (page 54).

Rhubarb and Raspberry

Cook separately and mix.

2 lb. rhubarb, 2 lb. raspberries or loganberries, $\frac{1}{4}$ pint water, 4 lb. sugar.

Add sugar, boil and pot. A good economical jam.

Rhubarb and Black Currant

The best of both world's.

2 lb. rhubarb, 2 lb. black currants, $1\frac{1}{2}$ pints water, mainly in the currants, $4\frac{1}{4}$ lb. sugar. Cook separately.

Mix, add sugar, boil and pot. Do not pass setting point.

Rhubarb and Orange

Fresh flavour with economy.

3 lb. rhubarb, 1 lb. orange flesh, juice and pith of 4 oranges, no water, $3\frac{3}{4}$ lb. sugar. (The pith should be in a muslin bag and removed after cooking.)

Simmer rhubarb carefully with orange and pith and peel, add sugar, stir well round, boil and pot.

STRAWBERRY

Strawberry

One of the delicious fruits but not an easy jam to perfect. Long cooking should be avoided or the fruit will be mashed down and lose colour. No acid or pectin.

4 lb. strawberries, 4 lb. sugar, no water, $\frac{1}{2}$ pint red currant or gooseberry juice.

Simmer carefully, stir frequently, add sugar and fruit juice, boil rapidly to setting but not fast and pot. Wait till practically cold before potting to ensure even distribution of fruit.

Strawberry and Gooseberry

See Gooseberry and Strawberry (page 54).

Strawberry and Raspberry

See Raspberry and Strawberry (page 58).

VEGETABLE JAMS

Selected vegetables make attractive economical and cheap jams. The best varieties are given on page 46.

GARDEN BEETROOT

Beetroot

This is quite tasty but needs acid, pectin and flavourings.

4 lb. beetroot, 2 pints water, 4 lb. sugar, rind and pith and juice of 4 lemons. (The pith should be in a muslin bag and removed after cooking.)

Wash beetroot, whole, unskinned and cook until tender.

Pull off skins and cut roots into cubes. Put back into pan to simmering, add 4 lb. sugar plus the lemon, boil and pot.

As flavouring, add during the final boil 2 teaspoonsful ground cinnamon or 2 teaspoonsful of vanilla essence.

Beetroot and Carrot

As above using equal weights of each and cooking separately.

CARROT

Carrot

4 lb. young fresh carrots (for preference), water to cover, 3–4 lb. sugar, rind, pith and juice of 4 lemons. (The pith should be in a muslin bag and removed after cooking.)

Wash and scrape and cut into ½ in. cubes. Place in pan with water to cover and cook until soft but not mushy.

The cubes can now remain as they are or passed through a sieve to make a pulp. To each pound add 1 lb. sugar plus the lemon, boil and pot and seal airtight.

Carrot and Beetroot

See Beetroot and Carrots, above.

CUCUMBER

Cucumber

4 lb. cucumber, 4 lb. sugar. To each pint of juice and pulp, add ½ oz. root ginger and rind, pith and juice of 2 lemons.

Peel and slice the cucumber, place in pan with the peel and pith and ginger (in a muslin bag) and cook gently to produce a medium pulp, then add the sugar and the lemon juice, boil and pot *OR* weigh, cover with equal weight of sugar and stand 24 hours. Bring to boiling and pot. The seeds can be sieved out.

MARROW

Marrow

This is a soft jam.

4 lb. prepared marrow in cubes or slices, rind, pith and juice of 4 lemons, 4 lb. sugar.

Cook marrow till firm tender and drain. Return to pan, add the lemon, 1 oz. bruised dried root ginger (in a muslin bag), bring to boil, add the sugar, boil and pot.

Marrow Ginger (A very popular concoction).

4 lb. prepared marrow cubes, 4 lb. sugar, juice of 4 lemons, rind and pith of 4 lemons and 1½ oz. bruised dried root ginger (in a muslin bag).

Cook the cubes gently so that they are still quite firm; steaming holds the shape best.

Place in a dish, sprinkle with the sugar, and leave for 24 hours and this will result in a substantial amount of liquid.

Return to the pan, bring to heat slowly to liquefy the sugar and cook until the cubes take on a yellowish transparent appearance but do not lose their shape. Setting is best tested by plate or flake. Pot hot and seal airtight.

This is a delicious jam. To save bother, the ginger can be in ground powder form at 3 level teaspoonsful.

Marrow and Pear

More flavoursome than plain pear.

2 lb. marrow, 2 lb. pears, 4 lb. sugar.

Peel and dice, de-seed the marrow and steam till firm tender. Peel, core and cube the pears and cook to soften, not to mash. Add together, plus sugar, rind, pith and juice of 3 lemons, 2 level teaspoonsful ground ginger, bring to boil slowly and pot. (The rind and pith of lemon and ground ginger should be in a muslin bag and removed after cooking.)

TOMATO

Tomato (Red)

4 lb. prepared tomatoes, 4 lb. sugar, no water, rind and pith of 2 lemons in a muslin bag.

Scald the tomatoes, remove skins. Cut in halves. Place in pan and cook for short while (3–5 minutes), sieve out seeds. Add sugar, bring to boil and pot. 1 teaspoonful of ground ginger can be mixed in.

Tomato (Green) (Mock Greengage)

As above but slightly longer simmering. Cook if possible in copper or brass pan.

PUMPKIN

Pumpkin

As marrow, but add sliced orange rind and pith of 2 oranges and 1 oz. bruised root ginger in a bag, and the juice of two oranges with the cubes. (See page 61).

Pumpkin and Orange

As marrow but add orange rind, pith (in bag) and juice of 2 oranges for 4 lb. pumpkin cubes. If bitter oranges are used, the ginger can be omitted.

4

Fruit Jellies, Conserves, Butters and Cheeses

What is a jelly?

It is a preserve of fruit and sugar which is clear and colourful and consists of the fruit without its attendant 'pieces' such as pulp, skins, seeds and pips.

A Perfect Jelly is:
1. Firmly set, able to hold its shape and quiver when taken from the jar.
2. Brilliantly sparkling in colour.
3. Clear right through, top and bottom.
4. Abounding in the natural fruit flavour.
5. Able to keep well in store.

A Bad Jelly is:
1. Stiff, hard or syrupy and liquid.
2. Dull and unattractive in colour.
3. Partly or wholly cloudy.
4. Lacking flavour, or of a foreign flavour.
5. Unable to store well (mouldy, fermented or crystallized.)

The Most Suitable Fruits

These possess a most distinct and attractive flavour and colour and have enough acid and pectin to set well: Crab apple, apple (cooking), bilberry, blackberry, black currant, cranberry, damson, elderberry, gooseberry, greengage, lemon, lime, loganberry, mint, orange, medlar, mulberry, plum, quince, red currant, rowan and sloe.

Tracing Mistakes

These are fully described under 'Jams' on page 36.

Here is the best method:

1. Select, prepare and cut up the fruit.
2. Weigh, place into pan and crush.
3. Add water, little or much.
4. Add acid if necessary, e.g. medlar.
5. Simmer to cook and extract juice.
6. Strain and test for pectin.
7. Add pectin if necessary, e.g. elderberry.
8. Return to pan, bring to boil.
9. Add sugar.
10. Boil rapidly.
11. Test to setting.
12. Add flavour and colour (if necessary), e.g. pear.
13. Remove scum.
14. Pot hot to top.
15. Seal airtight.

Special instructions (as above)

1. There is no need to take currants off bunch, or hull strawberries or top and tail gooseberries as these will be sieved later – what we want is the juice.
2. Weigh the pan and the fruit and squash down to break the fruit and help release the juice.
3. Juicy fruits, e.g. blackberries want ¾ pint water to 4 lb.; stiff fruits, e.g. apples 2–3 pints to 4 lb.; hard fruits, e.g. quinces 4–5 pints water to 4 lb.
4. Add acid – lemon juice or citric or tartaric acid (see page 24).
5. Simmer gently ¾–1¼ hours to cook the fruit and make sure *all* the juice is extracted.
6. Test for pectin. If low, add lemon pith and rind or pectin rich fruit, e.g. gooseberry (see page 53).
7. Strain hot in a warm kitchen at one go. The straining material should allow fairly free passage but stop all thick pulp. The best plan is to have a double strainer, one to remove the large pieces (e.g. strigs) such as a plastic sieve, coarse hair sieve or butter muslin and a second one beneath of flannel or felt.

   The wider the area of material the better, as sieving wants to be speedy. Keep it warm all round. It is wrong to press or force the pulp and to squeeze the bag as this is bound to lead to a cloudy jelly. All straining material should be soaked in boiling water to encourage the fruit juice to flow. To ensure brilliancy, an infusional earth such as Filtersel can be added to the juice before straining. (Instructions on the packet.) All the straining should be completed overnight (24 hours at the most), kept warm, and the jelly making proceeded with without delay.

A second extraction is possible where fruits are rich in pectin, e.g. red currants. The pulp left behind, after an hour dripping, is returned to the pan, water added to cover (i.e. half the quantity added at first), and simmered for ¾–1 hour, and then passed through the 2 sieved materials. The two extracts can be mixed together or the first one used for a special product and the second one to use early in the kitchen.

Pectin Test

The strained juice should be tested for pectin quantity and if deficient either simmered to draw off some of the water or have added a pectin-rich juice (prepared ready).

8. Measure the volume of juices, return pan to boil.
9. Add sugar according to recipe. If the pectin shows a good clot (see page 27) add 1 lb. sugar to 1 pint of juice: if a weak clot ¾ lb. to the pint.
10. Boil rapidly but setting point will be reached more quickly than with jam.
11. Test after 10–12 minutes boiling using the flake test (page 31) supplemented if necessary, with a sugar boiling thermometer reading at 220–221°F.
12. Add flavour or colour (harmless edible colours from your grocer).
13. Clear the scum off quickly.
14. Pot as quickly as possible in a warm kitchen or near a stove: if there is delay or a cold draught the jelly may start to set in the cooking pan. Pour slowly so that no bubbles are formed. Fill to the top.
15. Cover with a waxed tissue and seal airtight at once. Careful not to tilt the jars during cooling as they will upset the level and spoil the surface. It is not easy to give a ruling as to the weight of jelly produced because of the

varied quantities of juice extracted, but it is somewhere around 5 lb. for each 3 lb. sugar.

Pectin-based Jellies

This is a method where commercially-made pectins are used and the process differs slightly as follows:

1. Wash the fruit.
2. Crush, add water and simmer to extract the juice.
3. Strain juice as above.
4. Weigh juice and sugar separately.
5. Place in pan.
6. Cook rapidly.
7. Add commercial pectin (powder or liquid): see instructions on packet or bottle.
8. Heat to produce a rolling boil as directed (usually $\frac{1}{2}$–1 minute.)
9. Take from heat, skim, pot and seal.
   Around $3\frac{1}{2}$ lb. jelly is made for $3\frac{1}{2}$ lb. fruit and 3 lb. sugar.

Score card

Container Cover, label, date Cleanliness, wax circle	1
Colour	5
Quantity, texture Quality, consistency	6
Flavour	8
	20

JELLY RECIPES

All based on 4 lb. fruit: sugar in lbs. per pint juice and then proceed for the general method (page 65).

Apple (Crab or Cooking or Windfall)

4 lb. wash and cut up into medium slices, put in pan, with 2 pints water, simmer 1¼ hours, strain (can be double), measure, add 1 lb. sugar to 1 pint of juice, boil, test and pot.

To give flavour, the juice of 2 lemons plus peel coarsely sliced can be added with the cooking.

Apple and Quince

See Quince and Apple (page 71).

Apple and Red Currant

See Red Currant and Apple (page 72).

Bilberry

Good flavour and colour but needs both acid and pectin (suggest apple or gooseberry pectin). 4 lb. fruit, ½ pint water, citric acid (1 level teaspoonful), ¾ lb. of sugar to each pint of juice.

Blackberry (Bramble)

One of the most popular and deservedly so. 4 lb. washed blackberries, ¾ pint water, 4 tablespoonsful lemon juice (to provide the acid if berries are deficient) 1 lb. sugar to each pint of juice.

Blackberry and Apple

3 lb. blackberries, 1 lb. cooking apples, 1 pint water, no lemon juice. Then as above.

Black Currant

A most valuable jelly. 4 lb. washed fruit (on stalks), 2½ pints water, 1 lb. sugar. For economy, two extracts can be made using 1½ pint water at the first and then for the second cooking 1 pint water. Follow the recipe for 2 extracts (page 66).

Black Currant and Apple

This is useful to economize by adding a cheap fruit to one more expensive. 2 lb. currants (on stalks), 2 lb. cooking apples, cut into slices, 2 pints water, 4 lb. sugar. Simmer long to extract both currant and apple juice. Sets well so try it for setting after 8–10 minutes, then pot.

Cherry

A delicate but intriguing flavour and colour. Use ripe, red or black cherries (*see* Varieties, page 41). 4 lb. fruit (stoned), ¾ pint water, add 4 tablespoonsful lemon juice plus home-made pectin (suggest gooseberry). Simmer long to extract what juice is available. Sugar 1 lb. to pint.

Cranberry and Apple

2 lb. washed berries, 2 lb. cooking apples, 2 pints water. No need for acid or pectin. It makes a good set and a nice sharp flavour and colour. 1 lb. sugar to the pint. Simmer both fruits together. Test for setting in time.

Damson

An easy jelly and abounding in flavour. Two extracts can be made if desired (as blackberry). 4 lb. fruit, 2 pints water for 1st extract and 4 lb. fruit and 1 pint water for 2nd extract. Strain and add both together, add 1 lb. sugar to the pint of juice, boil to setting, pot hot.

Elderberry and Apple

Cheap, good and healthful. Can be domestic cooking apples or crab apples. Best to use apples because elderberry does not set well, 2 lb. elderberries from the stalk, 2 lb. sliced apples, each cooked by itself, water just to cover, 1½ pint. Strain juice, mix together, add barely 1 lb. sugar to the pint, boil, test and pot.

Gooseberry

4 lb. gooseberries (with head and tail), 2 pints water, 1–1¼ lb. sugar to the pint. Follow standard recipe. Two extracts can be taken, in which case use 1 pint water in each case.

The final colour will follow that of the ripe gooseberry (*see* Varieties page 41).

Gooseberry and Strawberry

See Strawberry and Gooseberry (page 74).

Gooseberry and Red Currant

A good setter. 2 lb. of each (unstalked), 1 pint water ($\frac{3}{4}$ pint if ripe). Make separate extracts. 1 lb. sugar per pint. Watch out for setting after 7–10 minutes, then pot hot as usual.

Loganberry

A vivid colour and fragrant flavour. Use fully ripe fruit (not overripe). To encourage a good set, add 2 tablespoonsful lemon juice before cooking. Otherwise simmer 4 lb. berries with $\frac{3}{4}$–1 pint water, strain, add 1 lb. sugar per pint, boil, test for setting and pot hot – the standard recipe.

Mint (Apple)

4 lb. sliced apples (green cookers), $2\frac{1}{2}$ pints water plus juice of 3 lemons plus 4 top tender sprigs of mint (or $\frac{1}{2}$ cup fresh chopped mint leaves in bag or finely chopped loose), all cooked to a pulp, strained, 1 lb. sugar added per pint, brought to boil, tested for setting, and pot. A bright green edible colour from your grocer helps to give a good appearance.

If an acid flavour is to be produced, then use the $1\frac{1}{2}$ pints water for a preliminary cooking and just before straining, 1 pint white vinegar plus another supply of mint. Bring back to boil, strain, test and pot.

Japonica

Free for the gathering. A fast setter although it is well to add 2 tablespoonsful lemon juice. 4 lb. washed and sliced fruit (mature not hard green), 5–6 pints water, simmer together long and steady, 1–$1\frac{1}{4}$ hours. Strain, add 1 lb. sugar to pint and pot, as standard. Makes a nice pink-orange jelly.

Muscat (Gooseberry)

4 lb. green gooseberries (not fully ripe), $\frac{3}{4}$ pint water, simmer to extract juice, strain, add 1 lb. sugar to each pint plus 4 elderflower heads immersed in the boiling jelly. Setting is easy then remove, test and pot – standard recipe.

Orange (and Apple)

A pleasant jelly of pronounced and distinct flavour. 5 oranges (sweet), 3 lb. cooking or crab apples, 4–5 pints water. Wash and cut into slices but without removing the orange pith. Add the water and simmer gently for 1–1½ hours until the whole is tender and the juice all extracted.

Strain, (may take some while, do not hurry) add 1 lb. sugar to each pint, boil rapidly 8–12 minutes to setting, pot and cover.

Plum Jelly

Wash 4 lb. strongly flavoured red Victoria or black plums (*see* Varieties page 42). Simmer in 1¼ pints water in which 3 tablespoonsful lemon juice have been added. Strain, add 1 lb. sugar to pint of juice, boil, pot and cover.

Quince

Perhaps the nicest of all for flavour, colour and consistency, and needs some acid, 4 tablespoonsful lemon juice. 4 lb. ripe quince, washed, cut into small cubes or slices and cooked with 4½ pints water and lemon juice in a covered pan until mashy and tender (1–1¼ hours) and strained.

A second extraction is of good quality using 2 pints water, and strained. Both extracts are added together, 1 lb. sugar to each pint stirred in, brought up to boiling, tested for setting (should soon be ready) potted and covered.

Quince and Apple

The quince and apple are highly complementary and possibly cheaper than quince alone. Cook 2 lb. of each separately, add together and carry on as standard recipe.

Raspberry

Another popular jelly, good for soothing sore throats if 2 tablespoonsful white vinegar are added as boiling is finished and just before potting.

It is not a good setter and 4 tablespoonsful lemon juice should be added, before simmering, to 4 lb. fruit. Hardly any water is used to assist the gentle extraction of juice. It helps to mash down the fruit. Then strain, bring to the boil, add

1 lb. sugar to each pint of juice in the pan, and boil hard to setting point.

Raspberry and Red Currant
See Red Currant and Raspberry, below.

Red Currant
An excellent jelly either as a confection or as a complement to meat: a good setter and a delightful colour. Wash 4 lb. ripe red currants (white currants can be used partly but will lead to a pink jelly) on the stalk, place in pan with 1 pint water and simmer gently until currants are broken down and mashed. Strain, measure, return to pan and boil, add 1¼ lb. sugar to each pint, boil to jell and pot and cover.

Red Currant (Concentrated)
A firmer and stronger flavoured jelly can be made by adding no water to the fruit: but simmer slowly, strain and drain, add 1¼ lb. sugar to 1 pint juice, bring to boiling and in 1–1¼ minutes it will be ready to pot and cover. To delay, setting could start in the pan because of the high concentration of acid and pectin.

Red Currant and Raspberry
Follow the standard recipe with equal parts of each fruit but cooked separately and the juices added. 4 lb. fruit, ¾ pint water (no acid), simmer slowly, sieve, measure, bring to boil, add 1 lb. sugar to each pint, boil hard and in a few minutes setting will be reached, pot and cover. This has a rather softer flavour than that made with red currants alone.

Red Currant and Apple
(To economize on the cost of currants.) 3 lb. red currants, 1 lb. cooking apples. Simmer separately. ½ pint water and 1½ pint water respectively, add together, bring to boil, mix in 1 lb. sugar to each pint, boil, test, pot and cover. An excellent setter, easy to make and of good value.

Red Currant and Gooseberry
See Gooseberry and Red Currant (page 70).

Red Currant and Rhubarb
  See Rhubarb and Red Currant, below.

Rowan (Mountain Ash)
  It is best to use apples as a complementary improvement and softening of the somewhat bitter flavour. There will be enough acid and pectin for a good set.
  Wash 2 lb. berries thoroughly, especially if gathered from a tree near a road and simmer with 1½–2 pints water. Wash and slice 2 lb. cooking apples and simmer with 1 pint water. Strain and mix both extracts together. Bring to boil, add 1 lb. sugar to each pint, boil rapidly, test for setting, pot and cover.

Rose Hip (with Apples)
  Can use equal parts hips and haws or all hips. 3 lb. apples (crab or cooking) and 1 lb. hips (or can be half and half). Wash both, add water to cover and simmer separately. Strain and mix together. Bring to boil and add 1 lb. sugar to each pint, boil to setting, pot and cover. It comes usually a dark red. If equal parts are used, add 2 tablespoonsful lemon juice to the hips.

Sloe (with Apples to soften the flavour)
  The set is excellent. 2½ lb. sloes, 1½ lb. cooking or crab apples. Wash and prick sloes, slice apples, add water to cover, 1 pint water and ½ pint water respectively. Simmer until tender, soft. Strain, mix, bring to boil, add 1 lb. sugar to each pint, pot and cover.

Rhubarb and Red Currant (or Black Currant)
  Rhubarb is not the best for jellies but it is cheap. 2 lb. sliced rhubarb (red stalks) 2 lb. currants (on strigs). ¾–1 pint water for black currants: ¼ pint for red currants or rhubarb.
  Simmer separately, black currants longest, red currants not so long, rhubarb shortest. The idea is to extract all the juice available. Strain, add together, bring to boil, add 1 lb. sugar to 1 pint juice, boil, pot and cover.

Strawberry
  Not popular but it has a 'gentle' flavour. 4 lb. strawberries,

½ lb. water, add 4 tablespoonsful lemon juice before simmering and home made pectin just before potting. Follow the standard method. 1 lb. sugar to the pint of juice.

Strawberry and Gooseberry (or Red Currant)

The 'other' fruit is used to give a satisfactory set. 2 lb. of each two fruits, simmer separately with ¼ pint water for strawberries, ½ pint for gooseberries and a mere trace for red currants. Strain, mix, bring to boil, add 1 lb. sugar for each pint, boil, test, pot and cover.

CONSERVES

This is a 'whole' fruit jam where the fruit is whole or halved and maintains its original shape, being permeated with sugar and suspended in a jelly or syrup of high sugar concentration – perhaps the most delicious of sugar-fruit confections.

There are two variations: (1) Where the fruit is treated with sugar prior to boiling, and (2) Where it is boiled in a syrup, this latter sometimes being referred to as a 'preserve'.

The Dry Sugar Method

For dry sugaring, the most suitable fruits are: apple, loganberry, marrow, melon, pear, quince, raspberry, rhubarb and strawberry.

Programme

1. Select and prepare fruit (fully as for normal culinary work).
2. Place in vessel between layers of sugar usually 1 lb. sugar to 1 lb. fruit.
3. Leave for 24 hours for the fruit juice to be extracted and the fruit itself to toughen.
4. Place in preserving pan (with any extras such as colour, flavouring or acid).
5. Bring to boil which will be complete (*a*) when there is a set (jell), or (*b*) when the syrup is thick. In both cases, the fruit should be a firm entity, either whole or part.
6. Allow to cool off slightly so that when potted the fruit will remain evenly suspended.
7. Seal airtight.

SPECIFIC RECIPES

4 lb. sugar to 4 lb. fruit unless otherwise advised. In every case, it is wise to add 4 tablespoonsful lemon juice in the preserving pan.

Apple

Cut to cubes which are put into a boiling syrup of 4 lb. sugar in 1½ pints water: boil for 40–60 minutes when the cubes will become clear yellow. Flavour with 4 oz. bruised root ginger, which should be in a muslin bag and removed after cooking.

Cherry

Use red cherries (May Duke, Morello or Flemish Red), stoned and treated whole or halved: 3½ lb. sugar, plus white pith and peel of 2 lemons in a muslin bag, removed after cooking.

Marrow

Ripe and firm. Cut into ½ in. cubes. Flavour with ginger (as above, Apples). 3½ lb. sugar.

Melon

Delicious, ripe but firm, any colour but deep orange is most attractive. Cut into ½ in. cubes, and add ginger and white pith of 2 lemons both in a muslin bag.

Pear

Another delicious one. Firm, ripe dessert pears are cubed or sliced and then sugared, but hard cooking pears must be cooked firm first. Add ginger and pith in a muslin bag. Can be coloured pink or a variety used which goes pink on cooking.

Pineapple

Into chunks: white pith used.

Quince

Cut into cubes and cook firm, then sugar, using some part of the cooking water as desired.

Raspberry

Fruit should be firm ripe, and evenly coloured. Add 2-lemon pith.

Rhubarb

Early red variety: white lemon pith. Colour red. 3½ lb. sugar.

Strawberry

Sugar, then boil for 3–4 minutes: put into basin for 8 hours and then boil again to reach setting or thick consistency. Add white pith of two lemons in a bag, and 2 tablespoonsful lemon juice before cooking.

The Boiling Syrup Method: (*a*) Rapid, (*b*) Slow

The best fruits are apple, apricot, blackberry, cherry, fig, grapefruit, loganberry, marrow, melon, nectarine, peach, pear, plum, pineapple, quince, raspberry and strawberry.

(*a*) *The Rapid Method*
1. Select, prepare and cut fruit into cubes or slices.
2. Place into boiling syrup 1 lb. sugar to 1 pint water (50%) and continue to boil.
3. Test with a jam thermometer to 218–220°F.
4. Take off heat and allow to cool for 15 minutes to plump up the fruit, stirring occasionally.
5. Bring to the boil.
6. Allow to cool down to form a skin.
7. Stir to ensure even distribution of the fruit.
8. Pot into hot jars.
9. Seal airtight.

(*b*) *The Slow Method*
(Superior fruit quality) in which the sugar is made to diffuse into the fruit cells.
1. Select and prepare fruit.
2. Boil in weak syrup 1¼ to 1 quart water (40%) just to cover until firm-tender but not squashed. (First boil).
3. Remove from heat and stand aside for 24 hours. Cool quickly.
4. Increase sugar concentration by 10% (adding 11 oz.)

5. Boil for 2 minutes (Second boil).
6. Stand aside again for 24 hours. Cool quickly.
7. Increase concentration by 10% (add 17 oz.).
8. Boil for 2 minutes – sugar strength now 60% and conserve; will keep well. (Third and final boil).
9. Remove from heat and cool to form skin.
10. Stir to distribute the fruit evenly.
11. Pot into hot jars.
12. Seal airtight.

The result is a fine quality conserve with the fruit plump, brilliant in colour and of a fresh fruit flavour.

Acid, flavour and colour, may be added as desired. Overboiling must be avoided or the colour may be darkened and crystallization occur in store.

SPECIAL HINTS

Berried Fruits

Two boilings only but the first syrup must be 60% so add the 3rd step sugar at the 2nd step.

Medium Firm Fruits

For peaches, plums and figs, follow the standard method. Prick plums to avoid bursting.

Hard Fruits

Apples, pears, quinces may need cooking in plain water first until firm-tender followed by a 50% sugar and a final 10%.

Syrup

If the level falls considerably, add boiling water (not syrup) up to original level.

If there is too much syrup, use it for cooking in the kitchen but the fruit in the jars should be covered with the syrup.

FRUIT BUTTERS

This is a delicious fruit preserve. It is a concentrated smooth paste which though stiff, spreads easily, its chief attribute being that it is free from skins, pips and seed. It is all fruit pulp and sugar, and this is most appreciated by those whose digestion may be upset by eating skins, etc., and also, for those whose dentures are not a too perfect fit!

The operation is simple and foolproof:

1. Wash ripe, sound fruit and cut up large fruits such as apples and pears; otherwise there is no need for strigging, topping and tailing, etc.
2. Weigh the pan (and spoon).
3. Put fruit in pan and water to cover.
4. Add acid if necessary (see page 24).
5. Simmer slowly until the fruit is soft.
6. Pass through a plastic, nylon or hair sieve (not metal) to exclude all but the pulp.
7. Weigh pulp.
8. To each pound of pulp add $\frac{1}{2}$–$\frac{3}{4}$ lb. sugar.
9. Return to pan and stir the sugar in.
10. Boil (not too fierce) for $\frac{1}{2}$–1 hour until the butter is semi-solid neither runny nor stiff. It must be 'spreadable' *when cold*.
11. Stir frequently or the thick mass may burn at the bottom.
12. Add any flavouring or colour and stir well in.
13. Ladle it hot into hot jars.
14. Seal down hot airtight.

The most suitable fruits for both butter and cheese recipes (which follow) are: apple, crab apple, apricot, black currant, blackberry, cranberry, damson, gooseberry, grape, loganberry, medlar, marrow, mulberry, peach, pear, plum, quince, rhubarb and tomato.

Adding Acid

It does help if the juice of 2 lemons (or $\frac{1}{2}$ teacup of citric or tartaric acid solution) is added at the commencement to each 4 lb. of fruit (see page 24).

Flavours

These, to suit the particular fruit, may be: apple – ginger, nutmeg, cinnamon, cloves; marrow – raspberry, strawberry, vanilla, orange; rhubarb – lemon, orange, raisin (stoned), damson; pear – ginger, clove; melon – ginger. The other fruits are not much improved but flavour can be included according to personal desire.

Sugar

White sugar if the pulp has a natural attractive colour or is to be coloured; brown sugar to give partly its own colour and flavour.

Finishing Point

This is determined by consistency *not* by setting point (which is not tested) realizing that the preserve will be thicker when set (cold) than when boiling (hot).

FRUIT CHEESES

The same fruits as recommended for butter are most satisfactory. This follows the operation of making a butter with the difference that $\frac{3}{4}$–1 lb. sugar is added to each pound of pulp and boiling is continued until the pulp is almost solid. The addition of acid as for butters is advised. There is no test for setting. It is then packed into small wide-mouthed jars or into moulds; rolled and cut into shape; sprinkled with caster sugar, cut into bars and coated with chocolate; used as a filling for chocolates and sweets.

It is delicious when served with game, poultry and other meats.

FRUIT PASTES

There is a cheese which has been dried to the consistency of almond paste and cut into bars, fingers, stars, circles, cubes, and so on. It needs no jar but is stored, wrapped in confectionery paper or foil in tins or boxes sealed with Sellotape sealing strip (No. 1401). Drying is done in a very slow oven, and frequently inspected.

5

Marmalades and Curds

A marmalade is a jam, jelly, thick syrup or pulp in which are suspended slices of fruit or peel. It is made from:

1. Citrus fruits, i.e. oranges, tangerines, lemons, limes, grapefruits solo or in combination, and
2. Non-citrus fruits, i.e. apples, apricots, peaches, pears and quinces.

CITRUS FRUITS (STANDARD OPERATION)

The operation is much on the same basis as the making of jam but longer cooking is needed to soften the peel. There is a wide choice of marmalades – thick, jelly, shredded and chunky.

Here is the operation:

1. Wash the fruit and scrub if dirty.
2. Take off peel, helped by soaking in hot water for 3 minutes.
3. Squeeze out juice, scoop out fruit pulp. Shred, peel, thin or thick; the thinner, the quicker will the pectin be released. Slicing is best done by hand with a very sharp knife. Place in cooking pan.
4. In a chunky marmalade, the white pith will remain adhering to the peel but in a jelly one, the pith is better removed and placed in a muslin bag along with the pectin-rich pips during cooking.
5. Add water, usually $3\frac{1}{2}$–4 pints to 2 lb. fruit (see recipes) or proportionately.
6. Add acid (to ensure a good set) as lemon juice (juice of 2 lemons), tartaric or citric acid, 1 teaspoonful per 2 lb. fruit.

7. Cook the fruit with the acid to soften both fruit and *peel*. This may take 1½–3 hours (*see* Recipes). It is important to cook the peel before sugar is added. Volume is usually reduced by half.
8. Add sugar usually 1½–2 lb. per 1 lb. fruit (*see* Recipes), i.e. 3–4 lb. per 2 lb.
9. If the fruit and peel have been fully cooked, the final boiling with sugar will not take longer than 15–25 minutes.
10. Test for setting (see page 30).
11. The scum can be a nuisance so skim the surface before boiling ceases.
12. Allow to cool down until a skin is seen to be developing, then stir round slowly.
13. Pour into warm jars, put on waxed circle, take to a clean cupboard or room to get quite cold (65°F. or lower).
14. Fix caps or seals.

Pressure Cooker Cooking

In order to reduce the rather long cooking 1½–3 hours in an open pan, the softening can be done in an ordinary pressure cooker although one is not able to do much at one time.

One pint water to each 1 lb. fruit is satisfactory. With the fruit and acid, usually 3 lb. fruit and 3 pints water can be put in without the rack. The lid is fixed with the vent open and with slow heating steam will issue. The vent is then closed, and pressure mounts to 15 lb. at which it is held for 15–20 minutes.

This should be sufficient to effect the necessary softening. The cooker is taken from the heat, allowed to cool for 10–12 minutes for the pressure to drop when the vent is opened and the lid taken off.

The fruit is then treated as per the recipe (pith, pips, peel, etc.) and either boiled with the sugar in the pressure cooker (open) or in an ordinary jam pan up to setting, skimming, cooling, straining and potting.

The above instructions are guidelines only, always consult the manufacturer's instruction book.

RECIPE DETAILS

Thick. Marmalades which contain peel, pith, flesh but not pips.

Seville Orange

A popular breakfast marmalade. Follow standard method. 2 lb. Seville oranges, juice of 2 lemons, 4 pints water, 4 lb. sugar or proportionately. Cook $1\frac{1}{2}$–$1\frac{3}{4}$ hours.

Chunky

2 lb. Sevilles, juice 2 lemons, 3–$3\frac{1}{2}$ pints water, 4 lb. sugar (half can be brown plus dark treacle 1 tablespoonful). Cut peel into small 'chunks' and leave pith intact. Add lemon juice and cook $1\frac{3}{4}$–2 hours until softened. Pass the pulp through a fine sieve, add the peel to it, add the sugar, boil to setting, skim, cool, stir and pot hot, cover cold.

Lemon

2 lb. lemons, $3\frac{1}{2}$–4 pints water, 4 lb. sugar. Follow standard recipe. Limes can be used in place of lemons giving a pale, crisp-flavoured product.

Grapefruit

2 lb. grapefruit, $\frac{1}{2}$ lb. lemons, $5\frac{1}{2}$ pints water, 4 lb. sugar. Cut peel medium. Leave in pith. Put pips in bag. Cook for 2 hours until peel is tender and volume reduced by about half. Take out bag of pips, add sugar, stir to dissolve, boil sharp to setting, half cool, stir, pot and cover cold.

Old English

2 lb. Sevilles, $\frac{1}{2}$ lb. lemons, 4 pints water, $4\frac{1}{4}$ lb. sugar (of which 1 lb. brown). Cut peel chunky (pith and pips in bag). Cook $1\frac{1}{2}$–$1\frac{3}{4}$ hours to reduce by half. Add the sugars, boil quickly to setting and complete as standard recipe.

Three Fruit

A good combination is 2 sweet oranges, 2 grapefruit and 3 lemons to a weight of about $2\frac{1}{2}$ lb., $4\frac{1}{2}$–5 pints water, 5 lb. sugar, not too much pith attached to peel. Cook slowly for $1\frac{1}{2}$ hours, add sugar and continue as standard recipe.

Four Fruit

The best flavour is got from 2 sweet oranges, 1 grapefruit, 2 lemons and 2 cooking apples. Wash and slice peel of citrus fruits, cover with water and cook for 12–15 minutes.

Peel and core apples and cut into half slices. Press out citrus juice and cut up fleshy part.

Add these together and simmer for 15–20 minutes, then add 4½ lb. sugar and boil to setting. Continue as standard.

Any combination of the above fruits can be used without upsetting the result.

Orange and Lemon

Follow standard recipe, prepare, simmer and boil all together. Use 3 lemons and 3 oranges, 5 pints water and 4 lb. sugar.

Seville and Sweet

A thicker marmalade, 4 Seville, 2 sweet, 4 pints water, 4 lb. sugar, 4 tablespoonsful lemon juice. Cook all together. Follow recipe of chunky marmalade.

JELLY MARMALADES

These differ from the thick marmalades in that they consist of a clear jelly in which is evenly suspended thinly sliced peel.

Seville Orange Jelly

2½ lb. Sevilles, juice of 2 lemons, 4 pints water, 3½ lb. sugar. The operation is in 2 parts (1) to produce the firm sliced peel and (2) to provide the clear jelly.

Scald the oranges, cut off the peel and the thick pith and slice the peel almost like matchsticks – even in length and size. Cook with 1 pint water for 1½–2 hours until tender and firm.

Cut up the fleshy parts and pith and lemon juice (pips in bag) in 2½ pints water and cook slowly for 1¾–2 hours.

Pour the liquid from the sliced peel, add to the fleshy pulp and pass through a fine sieve plus jelly bag taking about 15–20 minutes.

Put the pulp back into the pan plus 1 pint water, cook for 15–20 minutes and strain.

All the strained juice goes into the pan, bring to boil. Add 3½ lb. sugar, allow to dissolve, add the cooked shredded peel and boil hard to setting. Complete as standard.

Grapefruit Jelly

This follows the above recipe with two ¾ lb. grapefruit and 3 lemons of a total weight of 2–2¼ lb. For simmering about 4¼–4½ pints water will be necessary and 3 lb. sugar. Be sure to strain well to produce a clear jelly. This is a rewarding jelly of 'clean' flavour.

Tangerine Jelly

For the most delightful results and satisfactory setting, the tangerines should be produced as a jelly rather than a marmalade with the addition of lemons and grapefruit, e.g. tangerines 2 lb., two lemons and one grapefruit to total 2¾–3 lb.

Follow the jelly recipes but allow only tangerine shreds in the final product. The peel, pith and pips of the grapefruit and lemons are used in a bag during simmering but the pulp of these is added with the tangerine pulp plus tangerine shreds.

Tomato Marmalade

Quite economical, and tasteful; 5 ripe tomatoes, 4 lemons, ½–¾ pint water, 4¼ lb. sugar. Take off skins by blanching (putting into hot water), slice and put into pan. Extract the lemon juice and add to the tomato pulp. Slice lemon peel and put in bag with pith and pips; Add sugar to the water, bring to boiling. Put in the tomato slices and the 'jelly bag' and boil to setting, up to 25–35 minutes.

If shreds are required, cook the sliced lemon peel separately to tender and then add to the boiled tomato pulp just before potting.

Rhubarb Marmalade

Economy. 3½ lb. cubed rhubarb, 4 lemons, 1¾ pints water, 3¼ lb. sugar.

Follow the tomato recipe, preparing and cooking the lemon peel first (sliced) (plus pips and pith in bag) until tender. Add the rhubarb cubes and lemon and cook carefully until firm–soft. Take out bag. Put in the sugar to dissolve and boil to setting.

Ginger Marmalade

This flavour can be added by mixing in $\frac{1}{2}$–$\frac{3}{4}$ oz. ground ginger to 3 lb. fruit just prior to the final boiling.

Sugar-less Marmalade (*for diabetics*)

For long keeping this should be potted into metal-capped airtight jars and then sterilized to 175°F.

3 Seville oranges, 3 lemons, $1\frac{1}{4}$ pints water, 10 saccharine tablets (or an approved powder as per directions), $\frac{1}{2}$ oz. gelatine to each 1 lb. pulp.

Take peel (plus pith) from fruit and slice. Put into pan with pulp and water and saccharins and pips (in bag) and cook for 30–35 minutes until tender.

Add the gelatine dissolved in $\frac{1}{2}$ cupful of the warm juice. Pot and cover and sterilize if required to keep long.

CITRUS MARMALADE WITH PECTIN BASE

Either home-made, apple pectin (page 27), or commercial pectin can be used.

The simple steps are:

1. Wash, peel and shred 3 lb. fruit.
2. Place in pan with 1 pint water.
3. Cook for 10 minutes.
4. Add juice and pulp to cooked peel.
5. Cook for 20 minutes.
6. Add $5\frac{1}{4}$ lb. sugar and 3 lb. prepared fruit to pan.
7. Boil for 5 minutes.
8. Take from heat and stir in pectin.
9. Allow to cool and stir to distribute shreds.
10. Pot and seal airtight.
    Yield $7\frac{3}{4}$–8 lb.

MARMALADE FROM NON-CITRUS FRUITS

This is really a conserve except that the fruit is sliced and the syrup is strained; delicious.

Suitable fruits are apples, apricots, peaches, pears, quinces and among vegetables, carrots.

Here is the complete and easy operation:

1. Select, prepare and slice the fruit.
2. Place in basin with layer of sugar (1 lb. to 1 lb. fruit).
3. Leave for 24 hours for extraction and hardening.
4. Place in pan and bring to boiling and setting point (apple slices can be cooked in a muslin bag to stop breaking down).
5. Strain liquid through jelly bag to clear.
6. Put strained juice in pan and add slices.
7. Bring to boil and skim.
8. Allow to cool to form skin.
9. Stir to distribute slices.
10. Pot and seal airtight.

The precise sugar, lemon juice or acid quantities are of those shown under conserves (page 65).

Apricots require ½ teaspoonful citric or tartaric acid: peaches 1 teaspoonful: carrots 2 teaspoonsful to each 4 lb. fruit or vegetable.

Score card

Container Cover, label, date Cleanliness, wax circle }	1
Colour	5
Quantity, texture Quality, consistency }	6
Flavour	8
	—
	20

FRUIT CURDS

This differs from other preserves in that butter, eggs and sugar are usually used with the fruit. It is thus highly nutritious, has fine tonic properties and can be used as is a jam or in many culinary practices. The quantity of sugar is variable according to the desired sweetness or briskness of the curd. It is important to cook slowly in order to avoid any risk of curdling.

Apple Curd

Although not a good keeper, this curd is useful for filling cakes, tarts, etc. Wash, peel, core and slice 2 lb. cooking apples and simmer slowly in water to cover till fully cooked, when they are mashed to a pulp. Add 1 lb. sugar, a level teaspoonful of ground cinnamon, 2 eggs (beaten yolks) and 3 oz. butter. Place over moderate heat (do not boil), and stir until the curd is moderately thick. Pot hot and cover.

Apricot Curd

Rather expensive but delicious. Cook 1 lb. fruit (with only just enough water to stop burning) until soft and pass pulp through sieve. Place this in a double saucepan with 12–14 oz. sugar, (stirred to dissolve), the grated rind and juice of 2 lemons, 4 oz. butter and 4 eggs (beaten). Heat, stir to thickness; pot and cover – this follows the usual standard recipe.

Gooseberry Curd

This is made as Apple Curd above. The gooseberries should be green and simmered with ½ pint water and then added 3 eggs (all beaten lightly), 3 oz. butter and 1 lb. sugar: otherwise as above.

Lemon Curd

A recipe which originated many years ago and seems now to be accepted as standard, make use of 4 eggs, 4 lemons, 4 oz. butter and 1 lb. sugar. The butter, eggs, the finely grated rind and the juice of the washed lemons and the sugar are placed in a double saucepan or in a basin over water, heated and stirred to melt the sugar.

Gentle heating (not boiling) continues with stirring usually about 20–25 minutes until it becomes thick when it is poured into hot jars with waxed circles, allowed to cool, and covered then stored in a dry cold pantry.

Lemon and Apple Curd

This can follow the recipe for Apple Curd with the addition of the juice and shredded rind of 2 lemons.

Marrow (or Pumpkin) Curd

Peel and cut up the marrow to produce 1 lb. cubes, simmer till tender and discard the liquid. Extract the juice of 3 lemons and grate the rind finely. Place in a double saucepan with 12–14 oz. sugar and 4 oz. butter. Simmer and stir until medium-thick, appreciating that a curd when cold is much thicker than one which is hot. Pot and seal. If desired, 2 eggs can be incorporated. Margarine can be used in place of butter.

Orange Curd

A useful recipe is 4 eggs, 4 oz. butter, 10–14 oz. sugar, 3 oranges, and lemon. Follow lemon curd method.

6

Pickles, Chutneys and Ketchups

The high price of vegetables and of commercial pickles and chutneys makes it well worthwhile to produce one's own at home whether brought in cheaply on a surplus or produced in the garden or allotment.

Home processing is neither difficult nor costly and the resultant product is certainly equal to or more often superior to that made by a commercial firm.

PICKLE MAKING

Equipment

Most of it will already be available in the kitchen. The *preserving pan* or saucepan must not be of brass, copper or iron because of interaction and the subsequent unpleasant taste, but of aluminium, stainless steel, Monel metal or unchipped enamel.

Basins for brining can be of the same materials as those recommended for the pan and also of earthenware, plastic (provided it is not affected by acid, etc.), or glass.

The sieve must be of hair, nylon or plastic, not of metal. Butter muslin over a glass tundish or funnel is excellent.

Stirring spoons are best of plastic, wood or glass.

Scales should weigh in quarter ounces.

There is a wide choice of *bottles* and those made specially for vinegar-preserved products are recommended because they are so made and capped that there is no action of the vinegar on metal. These have metal or plastic caps, screw-down or clip-on, with a lining impervious to the action of vinegar.

Other useful covers are (1) a bung cork to fit the glass jam or other jars pushed down on to a sheet of stout greaseproof paper or ceresin with another sheet at top tied firmly with thin string, (2) a 'bottling' jar which has a glass cap, screw band and spring clip, (3) a cover of greaseproof plus wax-coated muslin, tied securely and (4) special preserving skin tied on tightly.

Whatever is used (and the special jars are far the best and safest), there must be neither chance of corrosion nor of evaporation, in the former case the metal is gradually destroyed and in the latter the product loses its edible value and becomes hard and distasteful.

THE SALT

The *salting or brining* of vegetables is for the purpose of extracting some of the water and carbohydrates from the tissues, making the pickles crisp and preventing the development of bacteria – all with the aim of ensuring successful preservation in store.

Block salt scraped to a powder is still preferred by many but the fine packet salt is considered a time saver, the sort which contains chemicals to stop caking may lead to the forming of a slight deposit or the clouding of the vinegar – a bad feature if the jar is to be exhibited.

The *standard brine* can be in *solution* (1 lb. salt to 1 gallon water or 2 heaped tablespoonsful to 1 pint water) or in a *dry powdered* form sprinkled between the layers of the prepared vegetables, usually at 1 level tablespoonful to 1 lb. vegetables.

Home-made pickles are of a brighter colour and more attractive in flavour than those made commercially because the latter are held in store until the processors are ready) in a brine for maybe 6–9 months when they are 'cured', becoming dark in colour, transparent and soft. This long curing is, neither necessary nor advisable from a home point of view.

THE VINEGARS

Vinegar is made by the fermentation of carbohydrates, e.g. home-made wine or malted barley, to alcohol and then from alcohol to vinegar encouraged by the action of acetic acid.

Bottled Vinegar

This is usually sold under the name of the manufacturer or bottler, is dependable and contains a minimum of 5–6% acetic acid. For good preservation, the vinegar strength in the final pickle should be at least 3·5% if it is to keep long and well.

Draught Vinegar (from a barrel)

Can be good or inferior but may have no more than 3% acid so that the final acid content is no more than 2% which will not keep the pickles well and probably allow mould or fermentation.

Bulk Vinegar

Usually low in price and useful for cooking or short-time preservation but it may have a low acid content and thus poor preservation power and could thus lead to the permitting of a cloudy covering liquid in the finished pickle.

Malt Vinegar

Is brown, shining clear, and made by the alcoholic fermentation of a malt infusion. It is most popular for pickling as it ensures an attractive flavour and a pleasing colour. Depth of colour in no way determines quality or acid percentage.

Wine Vinegar

Is usually made from inferior wines (alcohol to acetic acid) or from grape juice (sugar to alcohol to acetic acid). It is colourless, delicate of flavour, of top strength and is particularly valuable to use with colourful pickles for show purposes.

Spirit Vinegar

This is distilled from potatoes, grain or starchy vegetables or from yeast liquor, is of 5% or more acetic acid. Although of high-class quality it has no special advantage over other malt or white wine.

Cider Vinegar

This is much used in U.S.A. and is the conversion of apple

wine (alcohol) into acetic acid. It can be obtained at good shops and is not difficult to make at home.

Fruit Vinegar

Again can be an excellent home-made product – usually carrying at least 5% acid which is obtained if the sugar content (determined by a hydrometer) of the fruit juice is at least 12·5. When home-made wine has 'gone off' or 'sour', it can often be converted into quite good vinegar by adding 1 pint good vinegar to 4 pints of wine, stirring round and leaving exposed to the air but covered to keep dust out. Hold at 70–75°F. and do not destroy the film of 'mother vinegar' at the top. After 12 weeks or more the conversion should be complete.

Honey, below standard, can also be used.

White or Brown?

Generally brown malt should be used for top flavour and white wine or white malt for coloured products and for exhibition work.

Cold or Hot?

The choice is a personal one, as the keeping qualities are not influenced one way or the other. Shall we say 'cold', where the attraction of the pickle lies in its crispness, e.g. cabbage or cauliflower and 'hot' for soft vegetables, e.g. beetroot, cucumber or walnut.

Non-Brewed

This is a solution of acetic acid, coloured and flavoured, has a sharp taste but does not produce that well-known and well-appreciated pickle got by using one of the fermented vinegars.

SPICED VINEGAR

The age-old plan of putting whole spices in with the pickles is not favoured because the flavour is uneven; nor is the use of powdered spices because they dull the clarity of the pickle and often leave a deposit at the bottom of the jar.

It is much easier to pour on to the vegetables a specially-made 'spiced' vinegar. If this can be made early in the season and kept as wanted, so much the better for flavour, and this is made by putting the spice mixture into cold vinegar in a closed jar or bottle and leaving it, with occasional shaking or stirring up, for at least 8 weeks.

Preparing Spiced Vinegar

The more usual method for a quick result is to extract the flavour of spices by steeping them in hot vinegar following this recipe:

About 1½–2½ oz. of mixed spice (*see* Recipes) are placed in a muslin bag or in the top half of a double saucepan along with 1 quart of vinegar and brought up to boiling point, the lid being kept on all the time. The vinegar must *NOT BOIL*.

The saucepan is then taken off the heat and the spices allowed to stay in the hot vinegar for 2½ hours by which time the 'goodness' of the spices has been imparted to the vinegar, which is now fully spiced and is available for use at any time, keeping it in corked bottles in a cool place.

If it is cloudy, strain through a fine jelly bag. Put a label on the bottle indicating the type of spiced vinegar, e.g. universal, hot, sweet and so on.

Vinegar – cold or hot. Cold for crisp vegetables and hot (if preferred for soft vegetables). Hot means brought up to simmering and poured in hot, having earlier warmed the jars to prevent cracking.

SPICED RECIPES

These vary considerably. They can be bought ready-mixed at the grocer or made up to a formula and choice of which is given here, to each quart of vinegar:

Ministry of Agriculture	*'Grange' Spice*
¼ oz. cinnamon	¼ oz. cinnamon
¼ oz. cloves	¼ oz. cloves
¼ oz. mace	¼ oz. white peppercorns
¼ oz. whole pimento (all spice)	¼ oz. ginger
6 peppercorns	¼ oz. mace
	¼ oz. pimento

Sarsons Hot Spice
>1 oz. Mustard Seed
>¼ oz. chillies
>½ oz. cloves
>½ oz. black peppercorns
>1 oz. pimento

Special Vinegars

Some recipes advise the use of special vinegars which can be purchased at a speciality shop ready prepared or they can be made at home by steeping the leaves, petals, flowers, roots etc. in vinegar for 1–6 weeks, which is then strained, bottled, closely corked and stored in a dark place.

Some vinegars are given below, for 1 quart vinegar the first figure given is the quantity, the second the length of time in weeks:

>Celery: 1 quart fine chopped celery; 2 weeks
>Chilli: 100; 6 weeks
>Cucumber: 10 small, 3 onion; 1 week
>Horseradish: 3 oz.; 1 oz. shallots; 1 week
>Herb: 3 oz.; 3 weeks
>Mint: pack to fill quart jar; 3 weeks
>Onion: ½ cupful chopped; 2 weeks
>Rose Petal: 1 quart pressed down; 3 weeks
>Tarragon: 4 oz. leaves; 3 weeks
>Violet: 1 quart flowers pressed down; 1 week

PICKLE VARIETIES

There is a choice of:
1. Raw vegetable (cabbage, cucumber, onion)
2. Raw vegetables (mixed)
3. Cooked vegetable (carrot, turnip and other roots)
4. Cooked fruit (for all sweet fruits)
5. Piccallili (covered with special mixture)

Vegetable Pickle (Raw)
The operations are:

(1) Extract water by placing in a brine of 1 lb. salt to 1 gallon water (2 heaped teaspoonsful to 1 pint) or sprinkled with dry salt to cover.

(2) Leave for 24 hours (*see* Recipe).
(3) Drain off extracted liquid.
(4) Pack closely into jars to 1 in. of top.
(5) Pour on cold spiced vinegar to cover ½ in.
(6) Seal airtight
(7) Store cool, dry and dark.

1. RAW VEGETABLE RECIPES

Although especially good varieties are given, any vegetables surplus in the garden or available at a cheap rate could certainly be used successfully.

The months given are those when the vegetables are in the best condition and reasonable in price.

Cabbage (*Red*)

Wash, select hard and deep coloured heads, shred and cover with dry salt for 24 hours, drain, rinse off salt, pack fairly tightly, pour in cold spiced vinegar and seal air tight. Can be used after 14 days but goes limp after 10–12 weeks. (August–December).

Best varieties; Blood Red, Ruby Ball and Dwarf Dutch.

Cabbage (*white*)

Choose *hard* heads, wash, cut and shred. Dry salt for 24 hours, drain and rinse, pack tightly, fill with cold spiced vinegar and seal airtight. This is cheap and economical and can be used after 1 week as it loses its crispness in 8 weeks (August to November).

Cauliflower

Break selected heads of white close-knit curds into ½ inch pieces, brine for 24 hours, drain, rinse, pack, fill vinegar and seal.

Best varieties: Dominant, Danish Giant and Veitch's Autumn Giant. (July–September.)

Cucumber (Gherkin)

Follow standard recipe; cut small, brine 24 hours, pack in a layer or circle or upright (cut in sticks), ready in a week. (July–September.)

Nasturtium

Select fully green seeds when dry, wash, brine, drain, pack and seal. Do *not* use seeds of the Spurge (Euphorbia) which are poisonous. (September.)

Onion

Choose small hard-fleshed globular onions, brine before peeling for 12 hours, then peel, brine afresh for 24 hours, drain and rinse, pot and seal. Best to wait until the vinegar penetrates through the onion, 8–10 weeks. Varieties: Barla, The Queen, White Portugal, Silver Skin. There are varieties with red-tinged flesh; Red Globe and Blood Red. (July onward.)

A unique pickle is made by grating the onions, salting, drain and wash, pot, cover with white vinegar made pink with cochineal.

Shallot

Choose the smaller ones and follow as for onions. A good sort is Danish Yellow. (July and August.)

Walnut

Only immature nuts should be used before the shells have started to develop which is commenced at the end opposite the stalk. When the outer skin is pricked with a thin skewer, fork, or large needle, any shell can be felt, and such nuts should not be used. Brine for 5 days, pour off, brine for 7 days with fresh brine, drain, lay out on dishes until they turn black 24–36 hours, pot, spiced vinegar and seal. Ready in 6 weeks. Use plastic gloves as the brown stain is not easy to remove. (July and August.)

2. MIXED RAW VEGETABLES

These are a mixture of vegetables selected to balance one with a pronounced flavour, e.g. onions, with one with a delicate flavour, e.g. asparagus, or to improve or compliment one or the other.

The method is the same as that for 'Raw' vegetables (page 95).

Onion, Cauliflower and Cucumber

Peel the onions, break open the cauliflower and cube the cucumber. Mix together and dry salt for 24 hours. Drain, pack, pour in cold spiced vinegar and seal.

This is the popular 'trade' mixture. For show purposes, one should pack in an attractive pattern, rows and circles, and place in 2 whole red chillies (1 each side) to a ½ pint jar.

Cauliflower, Dwarf Bean, Marrow and Onions

This is an economical mixture to make use of dwarf or runner beans, late marrow and autumn cauliflower. The quantity of onions used will depend upon personal preferences.

Prepare by slicing the beans moderately thick, and cutting the marrow (or pumpkin) into ¾ in. cubes. Brine 24 hours; the marrow separately in dry salt.

Pack firmly in mixture. Follow standard recipe as for Red Cabbage.

Onions and Apples

An economy mixed pickle, with non-keeping small onions and apples (fallen). Peel onions, cube or slice apples and place at once into salted water for 3 minutes to stop them going brown.

Rather than salting; a preferred method is to use 1 level tablespoonful of salt to 1 quart vinegar to cover. Ready in 7–10 days.

Onions and Cucumber

Another economy pickle for surplus produce. Slice the onions, peel and slice or cube the cucumber, dry salt for 24 hours, drain, rinse, pack, fill spiced vinegar and seal.

Any variety of vegetable can be used to provide an alternative mixture.

3. COOKED VEGETABLE PICKLE

The vegetables used are those which are normally cooked such as beetroot, carrot, celery, gherkin, mushroom, parsnip, tomato and they make a most attractive pickle, e.g. orange carrots in white vinegar, macedoine of mixed cubes and slices of carrot, parsnip, turnip, beetroot – most pleasing to the eye; palatable to the taste.

The only difference between the production of these and that of (1) raw vegetable pickle is (*a*) no separate brining, (*d*) *cooking* in slightly salted water (1 tablespoonful salt to 1 pint water) until firm – tender (*c*) covering with *hot* spiced vinegar. This applies to all *root* vegetables.

Special Recipes
Beetroot

Wash and place in boiling salted water for 1–1¼ hours without breaking the skins. When still slightly warm, push off the skins, and cut the beetroot into ¼ inch slices.

Pack carefully into jars, pour on cold spiced vinegar and seal airtight. Use at once.

If it is intended to preserve it for some months, then it should be packed into 1 lb. bottling jars and filled up with boiling-hot spiced vinegar and sealed down with a glass cap and screw band.

Gherkin

(Immature cucumber, small ridge cucumber or 'pickling' gherkin).

Choose those no more than 3 inches long. Do not peel. Brine for 3 days. Drain, pack into jars, pour in hot spiced vinegar, cover lightly and leave for 24 hours in a warm kitchen.

Drain off vinegar, bring up to boiling, pour back into the packed jars, cover and leave another 24 hours. This is to result in the gherkins changing to a bright green and it may be necessary to repeat for a third time. After which, make up what hot vinegar is necessary, tidy up the packed vegetables, fill with hot vinegar, and seal airtight.

Good sorts are Prolific and Small Paris. (August to September.)

Mushroom

Peel, no brining, cook in casserole with *spiced* vinegar to cover until shrunk, pack in layers, cover with the same vinegar hot and seal airtight. (Any time when cheap.)

Samphire

This is a green succulent plant growing on the mud flats of the sea coast. It is delicious and health-giving and can either be collected or purchased 'infrequently' from the fishmonger or greengrocer.

It is best gathered young in late July and broken into 2 inch pieces and dry salted for 24 hours. It is then drained, cooked in plain vinegar to cover for a limited period so as not to soften or break down the pieces. (July–August.)

Packed horizontally round the jar and covered with plain (not spiced) hot white vinegar. It is a delicious product.

Tomato (Ripe)

Red or Yellow. Scald and take off skins of small fruit. No brining. Cover with vinegar as for green tomatoes and cook in oven for ½ hour. Pack carefully to keep the fruits whole and cover with hot onion vinegar. (When supplies liberal.)

Tomato (Green)

Slice if firm or halve if soft – dry salt overnight, drain, cover with vinegar plus one sliced onion and 1 tablespoonful of brown sugar to the pint, cook firm tender, pack in layers, fill up with the same hot vinegar. Seal airtight. (October onwards.)

Mixed

Any of the root or special vegetables described above can be mixed and prepared as for the standard recipe.

4. SWEET FRUIT PICKLE (or Spiced Fruit Pickle)

These are a luxury and especially useful for serving with hot or cold meats and all cheeses. They are not brined and are preserved in sweet or plain spiced (special) vinegar.

Suitable fruits are apple (including crab apple), apricot, blackberry, cherry, currant (black), damson, gooseberry, grape, peach, pear, plum and rhubarb.

Here is the Method

1. Select, wash and prepare sound, firm, ripe fruit; whole fruits pricked to avoid shrivelling.

2. Dissolve 2 lb. sugar to 4 lb. fruit in 1 pint vinegar (except for some special recipes given later).
3. Add the recommended spices (tied in a muslin bag).
4. Put all in a saucepan and simmer gently (keeping saucepan lid on) until firm-tender but not soft.
5. Drain off the vinegar carefully.
6. Pack the fruit into jars to within $\frac{1}{4}$–1 in. of the top.
7. Boil the vinegar – syrup until it is 'syrupy' (lid off saucepan).
8. Pour hot on to the packed fruit to cover $\frac{1}{2}$ inch.
9. Seal airtight without delay.
10. Store, dark, dry and cool.
11. Try to keep them 6–8 weeks before using.

N.B.: The spices must be suitable for fruits, i.e. aromatic and not those used for vegetable pickle.

Suitable *aromatic* spice mixtures are:

(*a*) Advised by the Ministry of Agriculture

$\frac{1}{2}$ oz. whole cloves	$\frac{1}{4}$ oz. root ginger
$\frac{1}{3}$ oz. allspice (pimento)	$\frac{1}{4}$ oz. stick cinnamon
Rind of $\frac{1}{2}$ lemon	

(*b*) The 'Grange' spice mixture is:

$\frac{1}{4}$ oz. mace	4 oz. cloves
$\frac{1}{4}$ oz. cinnamon	$\frac{1}{4}$ oz. ginger root
4 oz. pimento (allspice)	$\frac{1}{4}$ oz. coriander

The above spice quantities to 1 quart vinegar and 4 lb. sugar and 8 lb. stone fruit or pears or 1 pint vinegar and 2 lb. sugar and 4 lb. fruit and $\frac{1}{2}$ the spices quantity.

Special Recipes
Apple

$4\frac{1}{2}$ lb. apples (peel, core and slice), 4 lb. sugar, 1 quart spiced vinegar. Simmer all in saucepan to tender, drain, pack jar, pour on the hot vinegar boiled to a syrup to $\frac{1}{2}$ in. seal airtight.

Apricot

Halve, stone, pack without water and cook gently in an oven until the skins peel; pack and pour on thick hot spiced vinegar and seal: 3 lb. white sugar, $4\frac{1}{2}$ lb. apricots, 1 quart vinegar, white, to enhance colour.

Blackberry or Blackcurrant
4 lb. fruit, 2 lb. sugar, 1 pint special spiced vinegar. White unspiced vinegar, ½ oz. cloves, ½ oz. allspice (pimento), ½ oz. cinnamon. Follow standard method.

Cherry
2 lb. sugar, 4 lb. fruit, 1 pint *unspiced* white vinegar, 4 cloves, ½ oz. cinnamon, ½ oz. root ginger. Stone the cherries; best sorts being Morello, May Duke and Kentish Red. Follow standard recipe.

Crab Apple
3 lb. Crab apples whole and unskinned (cooked firm-tender with ¼ lemon and peel in water to cover fruit).

Put 1 pint malt vinegar (for flavour), 2 lb. sugar and ½ pint of the fruit cooking water along with spice bag into pan to boil, add the cooked crab apples and simmer gently until the syrup has become 'adhesive' (30–35 minutes), pack the fruit into hot jars, pour on hot syrup and seal.

A good spice is 2 in. stick cinnamon, 2 pieces ginger root and 2 cloves.

Damson
4 lb. fruit, 2 lb. sugar, ¼ lemon (and peel) 1 pint spiced white vinegar. Follow standard method.

Gooseberry
5 lb. fruit, 3 lb. sugar, 2 pints spiced vinegar. Use green gooseberries and simmer carefully to avoid squashing. Follow standard method.

Grape (Small outdoor)
4 lb. fruit, 2 lb. sugar, 1 pint of white spiced vinegar. Best to cook in slow oven first (see apricot) and then to pack and cover with hot spiced white vinegar.

Peach (fresh)
As for apricot. Skin with boiling water, blanch and halve.

Pear
4 lb. fruit, 2 lb. sugar, 1 pint spiced vinegar (brown malt

for flavour, $\frac{1}{4}$ lemon peel). Follow standard method. Excellent with pork.

Plum

Best are small firm-ripe 'cooking' plums; remove stones. 4 lb. fruit, 2 lb. sugar, 1 pint spiced vinegar, $\frac{1}{4}$ lemon (and peel). Follow standard method.

Rhubarb

3 lb. fruit, 2 lb. sugar, 1 pint spiced vinegar. Cut into 1 in. pieces. Follow standard method.

Cucumber (Sweet)

3 lb. fruit, 2 lb. sugar, 1 pint spiced vinegar. Cut up into convenient shapes. Cover in plain cold vinegar for 4 days; then carry on as method.

5. PICCALILLI

This is a mixture of vegetables in a thick yellow sauce which can be pungent, sour, sweet, hot or mild. It is most useful, appetite-rousing and popular. Any vegetables can be used, surplus or cheap, and deformed or diseased so long as the wholesome parts only are selected.

The most suitable vegetables are: beans (dwarf, runner and broad), cabbage (white or red), capsicum, cauliflower, cucumber, celery, gherkin, marrow, nasturtium seed, onion, shallot and tomato.

Preparation is to remove diseased or decayed parts, clean, peel, divide and cut up into small even pieces.

The 'Ministry' spice for a hot piccalilli as below is $1\frac{1}{4}$ oz. ground ginger, $1\frac{1}{4}$ oz. dry mustard, $\frac{1}{2}$ oz. turmeric, $\frac{3}{4}$ oz. cornflour or flour, 6 oz. sugar (white), 2 pints white vinegar.

For a sweet piccalilli; $\frac{1}{4}$ oz. ground ginger, $\frac{1}{2}$ oz. dry mustard, $\frac{1}{4}$ oz. turmeric, 1 oz. of cornflour or flour, 8 oz. sugar (white) to $2\frac{1}{2}$ pints white vinegar.

Standard Recipe

1. 6 lbs. prepared vegetables.
2. Place in wide, shallow dish and sprinkle with dry salt,

layer by layer, and leave for 24 hours (to draw out the water).

3. Drain, rinse and place in a cooking vessel, together with required quantity of white vinegar, spices, sugar and turmeric, depending on whether a hot or sweet piccalilli is required (put aside $\frac{1}{4}$ pint of the vinegar). Simmer until vegetables are either crisp or soft as desired, but not overcooked or squashy.

4. Blend the cornflour or flour with the reserved vinegar and stir into the cooked vegetables.

5. Bring to boil, stirring occasionally and boil for 3 minutes.

6. Pour into hot jars taking care to have an even distribution of vegetables in each jar.

7. Seal airtight.

An alternative is to strain off the vinegar from the vegetables after cooking, pack into the jars *and then* pour on the thick sauce to cover.

THIS IS A GOOD PICKLE

Cover No rust nor discolour; must have an acid-proof disc of cork, card, ceresin, or plastic.

Label and Date Important. Include name, date and any useful short details.

Clean Jar Smears and dirt on the outside indicate carelessness probably inside.

Grading Each piece must be of the same size and shape.

Colour Brilliancy is an attractive feature and leads to anticipation of a good pickle.

Packing Fill the jar by placing the pieces one between another with a piece of bamboo cane or a long-handled spoon. For exhibition; try to form a design, e.g. layers, contrasting colours, symmetric arrangement.

Condition Such fruit must obviously be clean, disease and decay free and there must be no odd pieces of skin, stalk or leaf.

Quantity In such a manner that the topmost pickle is covered by $\frac{1}{2}$ in. of vinegar and there is a $\frac{1}{2}''$ space between the vinegar and the acid-proof cap. An unsuitable cover will let air in to cause serious shrinkage.

Flavour Distinct of the vegetable, fruit or mixture. The spices should not be so strong or unsuitable as to mask the natural flavour. The vinegar must be piquant and not sour, musty, fermented, over-salt or over-sweet.

Clarity Vinegar must be brilliantly clear with little or no deposit or cloudiness usually caused by unsuitable brining or particles of suspended spices.

Texture Crisp products should be crisp, soft ones tender but not squashed or broken. Tough fruits e.g. damson may be due to the omission of pricking through the skins.

A pickle with these qualities may win in an exhibition but in any case it will contain a most attractive, nourishing and appetising product better than those offered in a shop and certainly for much less money.

Score Card

In order to make useful comparisons, the scores assist in evaluating.

Container Cover, label, date } Cleanliness, wax circle	1
Colour	5
Quantity, texture } quality, consistency	6
Flavour	8
	——
	20

CHUTNEYS

A chutney is a mixture of fruits and/or vegetables fresh or dried, cooked with sugar, spices and vinegar. It is a most rewarding preserve, quick and easy to make, uses cheap or low quality or glut produce and is a valuable supplement to many meat or fish dishes.

The most popular basic fruits are apple, blackberry, damson, elderberry, gooseberry, plum, rhubarb and tomatoes (green or red) and useful vegetables are beetroot and marrow.

These are the *basic* ingredients and to these are added products for their flavour, e.g. salt, spice, raisins, date, onion, ginger and those with sugar (demerara or brown) and vinegar (brown malt for flavour, white for light coloured produce) all cooked together, long and slow to produce this economical and satisfying mixture. Vegetables, rather tough, may well be cooked tender first in a part of the vinegar and spices.

Apparatus

The *cooking pan* can be of stainless steel, Monel metal, uncracked enamel, glass and aluminium but NOT of iron, brass or copper, which is acted upon to cause an unpleasant taste and peculiar colour.

Sieves should not be of metal other than stainless steel but better of hair, nylon or an acceptable plastic.

Jars. It is most important that chutneys are capped so that they will always remain airtight. Many chutneys improve with keeping but if air gets in, they sink down in the jar, become hard and unappetising.

A screw-capped jar with cork, ceresin or plastic lining is the only satisfactory cover.

The Standard Recipe

The Simple Operation is:

1. Select and prepare the fruits and/or vegetables.
2. Chop or mince fine. (This is considered the best way but some may prefer a coarse chutney with medium or large pieces).
3. Place in pan with whole spices in muslin bag or ground

spices (usually preferred) plus the other ingredients as per recipe e.g. onion, raisins, date, (not sugar) and just cover with vinegar.

4. Put lid on pan and simmer gently until all the ingredients are soft. The secret is slow and long cooking may be for 1–4 hours.

5. Dissolve the sugar in the remaining vinegar and add to the cooked lot.

6. Cook gently (lid off pan), stir frequently until the consistency is that of jam (remembering that chutney when it cools becomes thicker than when it was hot).

7. Fill up without delay into hot jars to $\frac{1}{2}$ in. of top and seal airtight.

8. Label and store away in a cool, dark, dry place.

Special Recipes

These can always be adjusted to be hot, mild, sweet, sharp by varying of the amount of spice, sugar, etc. (page 100). Spoonfuls mean 'level'.

Apple (6 lb.), onions 1 lb., sultanas 1 lb., salt 1 oz., sugar 3 lb., vinegar 3 pints, 1 oz. ground ginger, $\frac{3}{4}$ teaspoonful cayenne. Yield: 10–11 lb.

Beetroot (4 lb. cooked), onions $\frac{1}{2}$ lb., raisins (or sultanas) 1 lb., salt $\frac{1}{2}$ oz., white sugar $\frac{1}{2}$ lb., white vinegar 1 pint, 6 each peppercorn and cloves, 1 tablespoonful pimento.

Blackberry (6 lb.), apples $1\frac{1}{2}$ lb., onions 2 lb., 3 oz. salt, 2 lb. brown sugar, 2 pints brown malt vinegar, 2 oz. ground ginger, 1 teaspoonful cayenne, 2 tablespoonsful mustard, $1\frac{1}{2}$ teaspoonsful powered mace. Pips should be removed by passing the cooked blackberries through a sieve. Yield: 8–9 lb.

Damson (3 lb.), apples $1\frac{1}{2}$ lb., onions 1 lb., sultanas 1 lb., $1\frac{1}{2}$ oz. salt, $\frac{1}{2}$ lb. white sugar, 2 pints white vinegar, 1 teaspoonful pimento, $\frac{1}{2}$ teaspoonful mustard (can be omitted), 1 teaspoonful ground ginger, $\frac{1}{4}$ teaspoonful each cayenne and mace. Remove stones. Yield: 5 lb.

Elderberry (3 lb.), onions $\frac{1}{2}$ lb., sultanas 4 lb., 1 oz. salt, $\frac{1}{2}$ lb. sugar, 1 pint vinegar, 1 teaspoonful each pimento, cinnamon, cayenne and ground ginger. Use berries just ripe, not over ripe. Yield: $3\frac{1}{2}$–4 lb.

Gooseberry (3 lb.), onions ½ lb., sultanas ½ lb., salt ¾ oz., 1 lb. sugar, 1½ pints vinegar, 1 tablespoonful each pimento and ground ginger, ¼ teaspoonful cayenne. Half the vinegar can be tarragon vinegar. Yield 4–4½ lb.

Marrow (4 lb.), apples 1½ lb., onions 1 lb., salt 2 oz., sugar 1 lb., sultanas 4 lb., vinegar 3 pints, 2 tablespoonsful each peppercorns, mustard seed and cut up ginger root. Yield: 6½–7 lb.

Plum (4 lb.), follow damson recipe but with 2 pints vinegar, 1 oz. salt and ½ lb. chopped stoned raisins in place of sultanas. Yield 4½–5 lb.

Rhubarb (4 lb.), onions 1 lb., sultanas or raisins 1 lb., ½ oz. salt, 1½ lb. sugar, 1½ pints vinegar (1 lb. apples can be added), 1 tablespoonful each ground ginger and pimento and if desired of curry powder. Yield 5–6 lb.

Tomato (*Green*) (4 lb.), apples 1 lb., onions ¾ lb., sultanas ¾ lb., salt ½ oz., brown sugar 1 lb., vinegar 1¼ pints, 1 tablespoonful each mustard seed and root ginger (in bag) and ¼ teaspoonful cayenne. One dessertspoonful curry powder can be added if desired. Yield 6–7 lb.

Tomato (*Red*) (4 lb.), onions ¼ lb., salt ½ oz., white sugar ½ lb., white vinegar ½ pint, 1 level teaspoonful each cayenne, cloves and ginger (or mace). Yield 3½–4 lb.

Indian chutney, apples 4 lb., onions ¼ lb., sultanas 2 lb., salt ¾ oz., sugar 2½ lb. (soft brown), vinegar 2 pints (brown malt), 2 oz. ground ginger, 1 teaspoonful cayenne, and 1 oz. ground mustard.

Notes: Slight variations in the amount of sugar, onions and spices serve to make an adjustment particularly attractive to an individual. Sultanas can be replaced by raisins, currants or dates. Onions can be partly or wholly replaced with shallots. Garlic – be wary even with a few cloves. Dried fruit can be used in place of fresh but a ¼ of the sugar omitted. Colourful fruits demand white sugar and white vinegar. Hot chutneys require (4 lb. fruit), 1 teaspoonful each mustard and ground ginger and ½ teaspoonful cayenne pepper and ¼ oz. curry powder.

The consistency can be varied at the final cooking, longer to thicken and adding ¼ pint vinegar if too thick.

This is a Good Chutney

Cover airtight with a cork, ceresin, plastic or some vinegar-lining beneath the metal cap.

Label and Date　Most helpful but often omitted. Date and variety and useful details.

Cleanliness　No dirt or rust on caps, no smears on glass inside or outside.

Packing　To within $\frac{1}{2}$ in. of cap. Stored warm and with an air-loose cover, a chutney will lose one-third of its volume in 10 weeks and become dry and unpleasant.

Colour　The more brilliant, the more attractive: to make use of the natural fruit or vegetable colour: even colour all through.

Preparation　Careful mincing and chopping, etc.

Texture　Soft, mellow and even, with all produce blended. Skins should be soft and no hard particles. On the other hand, where a chutney is preferred in which the pieces are easily distinguished, so well and good!

Flavour　Distinct, pleasing, lively and balanced: appetite-boosting and enhances a cold meal. Much depends upon a person's own fancy. Must never be mouldy, musty, sour, bitter, fermented or excessively hot or sweet.

Score card

Container	
Cover, label, date }	1
Cleanliness, wax circle	
Colour	5
Quantity, texture }	6
quality, consistency	
Flavour	
	8
	—
	20

SAUCES

A sauce is a semi-liquid chutney that is made from the same type of ingredients but after the preliminary cooking (and before adding the sugar, salt and part vinegar), the mass is sieved so as to produce a smooth puree which when prepared further (see below) will result in a delicious and wholesome sauce of great value in the kitchen.

The most suitable fruits are apple, blackberry, red currant, damson, elderberry, plum, rhubarb and tomato.

The Standard Method

1. Select, prepare by cutting into small pieces, cubes or slices.
2. Cook to soften thoroughly.
3. Strain through hair sieve or muslin.
4. Place in pan and add the sugar, salt, vinegar and spices (in muslin bag) or use spiced vinegar.
5. Cook gently until the mixture is of the consistency of thick cream (remembering that it will get thicker when cold. It must be free to pour out of the bottle.)
6. Pour into hot bottles without delay (bottles see page 11) and seal airtight.
7. Store in a dry, cool, dark place.

Special Recipes

Apple (2 lb.), sugar $3\frac{1}{2}$ teaspoonsful, $\frac{1}{2}$ pint water (preferably soft), 1 oz. butter. Cut apples fine, put all in saucepan and simmer until the mixture is soft. To improve smoothness, the apples should be beaten or pressed. This will keep safely if put into warm jars and sterilized at 180°F. for $\frac{1}{2}$ hour and then sealed airtight.

Blackberry (4 lb.), apples 1 lb., onions $\frac{1}{2}$ lb., salt 2 oz., sugar $1–1\frac{1}{2}$ lb., vinegar 2 pints, 1 level teaspoonful each cinnamon, pimento, ground ginger and mace.

Damson (4 lb.), onions $\frac{1}{2}$ lb., raisins $\frac{1}{4}$ lb., salt $1\frac{1}{4}$ oz., white sugar $\frac{1}{2}$ lb., white vinegar $1\frac{1}{2}$ pints, $\frac{1}{4}$ oz. each ground ginger, pimento and mace and 2 level teaspoonsful each peppercorns and chillies (and 1 teaspoonful mustard if desired).

Cut up damsons, remove stones, slice onions, stone raisins, add the spices and $\frac{3}{4}$ pint vinegar and cook slowly until soft (25–35 minutes). Sieve the pulp, add the salt, sugar and ¾ pint vinegar and cook very slowly until creamy (50–65 minutes). Bottle hot and cover at once.

Elderberry (4 lb.), onions 4 oz., salt 1¼ oz., sugar 1–2 lb. according to preference, vinegar 1 pint, 1 level teaspoonful each cinnamon, pimento, ground ginger and cayenne. Excellent with fish.

Plum   Follow Damson recipe, currants in place of raisins. Use blue plums if possible.

Rhubarb (4 lb.), onions 3 lb., salt ¾ oz., sugar 2 lb., brown malt vinegar (for flavour) 2 pints, 1 teaspoonful each peppercorns, chillies, ginger, pimento (and if you like curry powder, see Chutney recipe).

Cut up, cook all together except the sugar, for 1¼–2¼ hours. Sieve, add sugar and cook again until medium-thick. A well-flavoured and cheap sauce.

Tomato (*Red*) (4 lb.), onions ½ lb. (if desired), salt ½ oz., sugar ½ lb. (to cheapen add also 1½ lb. apples), white vinegar ½ pint, 1 level teaspoonful each cloves, ginger and mace. A popular sauce for use at any time.

Tomato (*Yellow, ripe*)   These make a unique sauce with the above recipe with the apples but not the onions.

Tomato (*Green, unripe*) (4 lb.), apples 1½ lb., onions ¼ lb., salt 1 oz., sugar 1 lb., vinegar 1 pint, 1 dessertspoonful celery seed (if desired) and 1 teaspoonful each mustard seed, peppercorns and root ginger (in bag). Excellent flavour and a good way to use up the end-of-season unripe fruit.

N.B.: Tomato sauces are not usually good keepers and they should be sterilized at 180°F. for 30 minutes and then sealed airtight with screw caps (special bottles can be purchased.)

Horseradish Sauce   This is a special recipe as follows – (1) Scrape, grate or mince plump juicy horseradish root and without delay, (2) Place in a boiling solution of brine, 1 level teaspoonful salt to 1 pint water, for one minute, (3) Drain and pack in jars. (4) Cover at once with boiling white vinegar. (5) Seal airtight.

It is better not to add cream until the sauce is to be

used, in which case 1 tea cup cream and 1 level teaspoonful sugar is mixed in with each heaped dessertspoonful of horseradish (in vinegar).

This is a Good Sauce

Cover Airtight, clean and with a vinegar-proof lining.

Colour Bright, not dull, cloudy or streaky.

Texture Even and smooth all through with no pips, peel, skins or lumps. No free liquid.

Consistency As a sauce, semi-soft: to pour slowly without undue shaking but not to run out in a thin stream.

Flavour Most important. Preferably neither over-hot, sweet or salty: no mould, mustiness, bitterness, neither sharp nor irritant.

The 'Score Card' of points is similar to that for chutneys.

KETCHUPS

A ketchup is a thin 'sauce' which pours readily from a bottle, the thicker parts of the pulp have been sieved out. If the consistency of a ketchup is preferred to the thicker texture of a sauce, then the sauce recipes as given here can be adjusted so that (*a*) the fine portions are strained out for the ketchup and (*b*) the thicker part used as a chutney.

Sterilizing

As many of these ketchups are likely to ferment in store (especially those with little acid such as tomato, mushroom and walnut) it is a safeguard to sterilize by heating with loose caps in a water-bath for 15 minutes at 180°F. (simmering) and then screwing down each jar at once.

Spiced Vinegars

The recipes for these are given in page 93. If it is preferred to add separately then be guided by the spice formulas under chutneys and sauces, page 105.

The popular ketchups are those made from apple, blackberry, damson, elderberry, gooseberry, mushroom, tomato and walnut.

Apple (4 lb.), onions ½ lb., salt 1 oz., sugar ½ lb., spiced

FIG 10. A good home-made sterilizer is a vessel deep enough to allow for covering the bottles to the caps with water, and has a false bottom of wire netting to stop the bottles cracking at the bottom.

vinegar 1 pint. An easy method is to chop the apples and onions fine, place in a pan with the salt and spiced vinegar and cook long and gentle until the pulp is in a finely mashed state.

Pass this through a fine hair sieve, add the sugar, stir well in and boil for 5 minutes. Fill hot into hot bottles and sterilize.

Blackberry (4 lb.), salt $\frac{1}{4}$ oz., sugar $\frac{1}{2}$ lb., spiced vinegar $1\frac{1}{2}$ pints. Just cover the blackberries with water and simmer until well cooked. Pass through fine sieve to exclude the pips. Add to the salt (if desired), sugar and spiced vinegar and boil for 5 minutes. Bottle hot and sterilize.

Damson (4 lb.), salt ¼ oz., sugar 1 lb., spiced vinegar 1¼ pints. Follow damson recipe. Excellent with cold meats.

Elderberry (4 lb.), salt ¼ oz. onions, ½ lb., (sugar ½ lb. if a sweeter ketchup is preferred). Simmer the fruit with the 1½ pints spiced vinegar until all the juice has been extracted, strain, add the salt and onions and boil for 4–5 minutes. Take out the onions, bottle, cap hot and sterilize.

Gooseberry (4 lb.), sugar 2 lb., spiced malt vinegar 1 pint. Cook all together for an hour, strain and bottle hot.

Mushroom (most popular) (4 lb.), salt 4–5 oz., one small onion chopped fine, spiced vinegar 1 pint.

Skin and mince the mushrooms and stalk (open ones best), sprinkle with salt and leave for 2–3 days stirring frequently.

Place all ingredients and liquor in pan and cook gently for 1½ to 2 hours. Strain, bottle and sterilize.

Tomato (*most popular*) (4 lb.), onions ¼ lb., salt ½ oz., sugar 6 oz., apples ½ lb., spiced vinegar ¾ pint.

Slice tomatoes, onions and apples and simmer together, stirring frequently to avoid burning, until all the pulp has disintegrated and the maximum liquid has been produced. Strain, add to sugar, salt and spiced vinegar and boil carefully for 5 minutes: bottle hot and sterilize.

Walnut (*another popular one*) Cut in half and crush 70 soft green walnuts as used for pickling. Place in jar with 6 oz. chopped onions or shallots, 6 oz. salt and 3 pints of boiling spiced vinegar. Stir well to dissolve the salt and mix all well together and allow to stand for 5 days stirring each day.

Then pour the liquid part through a fine strainer, simmer for 1 hour, bottle and sterilize.

Notes: The spices may vary according to taste but they should not be so profuse that the flavour of the fruit is masked.

The ideal ketchup is a thin, bright, flavoursome product of extreme value for cold and hot meats, game and fish.

PICKLING, CHUTNEY AND SAUCE FAULTS

Cloudy Liquid

Use of poor quality vinegar low in acid: failure to cook (as per recipe): early deterioration through lack of proper procedure, e.g. short brining period or use of a low salt brine: presence of ground spices probably of poor quality.

Shrinkage in Jar

Evaporation in warm store: loose cover or use of one which is not airtight: careless packing so that vegetables sink down and leave spaces.

Loose Vinegar

Often occurs with chutneys and sauce which have not followed a satisfactory recipe or which have not been cooked for a sufficient length of time to ensure complete integration.

Tough Fruits

e.g. damsons and plums. Fruit should be pricked to allow vinegar to permeate right through. Fruits are hard and almost 'raw'.

Colour Change

In chutneys and sauces, there may be a ¼ or ½ inch layer which is of darker colour than that beneath. This may be due to air contamination, to short cooking, warm or long storage.

Bad Colour

Especially in tomato sauce is usually due to darkening through the use of brown sugar and brown malt vinegar or to some over-cooking after sugar is added.

7

Fruit Bottling

With the never-ending succession of price increases and in some cases the offering of produce of inferior quality, it is obviously a sensible plan to preserve our own fruit by bottling, a method in which the fruit is packed into bottles or jars to be entirely safe for later consumption and at the same time is of the colour, flavour and texture of the fresh fruit.

Although there is nearly a score of methods, there are two to be recommended; one, the 'water bath' method which preserves the features of the fresh fruit as near as possible and two, the 'oven method' which costs practically nothing and yet gives good results.

THE WATER-BATH METHOD

The easy to follow operations are:

1. Provide clean, tested, bottling jars with screw cap or spring cap cover either of metal or glass.
2. Prepare clean, disease-free fruit.
3. Pack firmly in the bottles.
4. Fill right to the brim with cold sugar syrup (preferable) or cold water.
5. Put on the cover but only partly fixed so that heated air can escape.
6. Place in sterilizer.
7. Heat to the correct time and temperature (important).
8. Remove from hot water and fix the covers right down at once.
9. Allow to cool and test for sealing.
10. Store away in a cool, dark, airy place.

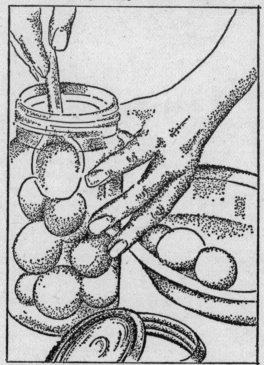

FIG 11. Packing large fruits such as plums, apricots, pears and peaches with a long-handled wooden spoon so that each fruit is packed down close to another. To make packing easy, run cold water in to make the fruits 'slide down'.

So simple, now for some details.

1. The bottles must be of the special type (e.g. Kilner, Sutcliffe, Fowler-Lee, Porosan) which have a definite airtight seal and they can be in ½ lb., 1 lb. and more commonly 2 lb. The glass or metal surfaces must not be broken or bent and the rubber ring must be fully elastic.
2. The fruit must be firm-ripe, fresh and if gritty and dirty it must be washed.
3. It must be packed tightly (without breaking) in the bottles with the aid of a long-handled, packing spoon or

FIG. 12. Filling the jar packed to the top with gooseberries with cold water or syrup prior to fitting the rings and caps and sterilizing.

a piece of bamboo cane 12 in. long, starting from the bottom of the jar and packing in layers to the top. It may be necessary to cut large fruits in half, in slices, in rings, in cubes or in stricks. It is easier to pack a bottle which is wet inside.

4. After packing, the jar is filled to the top with a covering liquid. This can be cold water or syrup. The fruit keeps well in water but its texture and flavour is much better held if a cold syrup is used of $\frac{1}{2}$ lb. sugar to the pint.

Sour plums or strawberries require 1 lb. sugar to the pint; damson, loganberries, raspberries and pears $\frac{3}{4}$ lb. to the pint.

Honey can be used at the ratio of 1 part of honey to 1 part of water (by volume) and treacle at one pint to 4 pints of water.

5. After filling, put on the cover partly, the screw band half unscrewed and the spring clips fitted half-way down.

6. Sterilising is done by placing the packed and filled bottles in a special sterilizer, but any vessel will do which is deep enough to allow the bottles to be almost covered with water but it must have a false bottom upon which the bottles stand, to avoid cracking. This false bottom can be of pressed down wire netting (the best), cardboard, wood or stout perforated zinc.

7. Sterilizing is done by heating the water slowly so that in $1\frac{1}{2}$ hours (and not before) the water temperature is 165°F. at which it is held for 10 minutes. The exceptions to this rule are for halved and stone fruit, unripe plums and for the larger bottles holding 3 lb. hold a water temperature of 165°F. for 20 minutes. For black, red and white currants and cranberries, the temperature should be 180°F. for 15 minutes; for cherries 190°F. for 10 minutes; for pears and quinces 190°F. for 20 minutes and for tomatoes boiling, i.e. 212°F. for 30 minutes. A floating dairy thermometer will register the temperatures.

8. When sterilization is completed, each jar should be removed from the hot water by the use of bottle tongs or with a dry cloth folded to 3 inch width, passed round the hot jar and held at the junction. As each is removed, the covers are fitted, screw band right down, spring clips pressed down and convex covers snapped down concave.

9. Stand the hot jars on a wooden surface, for a cold enamel or steel one will encourage cracking of the jar bottoms.

10. When quite cold, test for sealing. The screw band is removed and the glass or brass cap should be held firmly by the vacuum; the spring clip taken off leaves the cap held in position. The snap-cap has to be left alone.

11. Wipe the outside of the bottles and store away cool, dry, dark, airy and frost-free.

This method will keep fruit as near as possible in colour, flavour and texture to the fresh fruit.

OVEN METHOD (DRY PACK)

This is a quick method, at practically no cost.

1. Provide some clean 1 lb. or 2 lb. (best) jam jars which are level across the top and free from flaws or cracks.
2. Choose and prepare the fruit.
3. Pack closely to the brim.

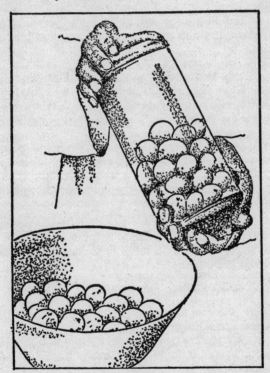

FIG. 13. Packing small fruit such as gooseberries by jarring the bottle down on the hand, doing this several times as it is being packed.

4. Add no liquid yet.
5. Lay patty pans, or saucers or lids upon the top of the jars to prevent fruit scorching.

6. Place upon an oven shelf but not touching one another.
7. Heat the oven gradually to 240°F. so that in 1 hour the fruit has changed colour and has shrunk down slightly in the bottles.
8. It is usually sufficient to heat only for $\frac{3}{4}$ hour with berried fruits but tomatoes and pears $1\frac{1}{2}$ hours.
9. Have ready boiling water or syrup ($\frac{1}{2}$ lb. sugar to the pint).
10. Take each bottle out of the oven *separately* with bottle tongs or a dry dish cloth and fill up to within $\frac{3}{4}$ in. of the brim.
11. Fix the cover *airtight*. The cheapest but excellent cover is a treble thickness of greaseproof paper, each piece stuck together with hot water starch and firmly stuck down over the rim of the filled bottle. Take care not to let the bottle fall over to dampen the inside of the greaseproof paper covers.

    Other good covers are a special sealing skin, a cork covered with wax, a press-on cap or any of the special bottling jars as used in the method given above.
12. Be sure to store away in a dry and mouse-free place and preferably dark and cool.

This is a cheap excellent, and quick method, requiring the minimum of bought-in apparatus and the fruit can be used neat as a salad or in pies, tarts, flans, sundaes or as fresh fruit would be prepared.

BOTTLING FAULTS AND HOW TO AVOID

Loose seal Flaw in fittings; crack in jar; bad rubber ring; failure to screw down fully when hot.

Bottle crack Failure to use a false bottom in the sterilizer, standing in cold draught after removal from hot water in sterilizer.

Failure to keep Insufficient heating, too low, too short; undiscovered crack or fault in sealing allowing air to get in.

Colour fading Storing on a sunny shelf.

Bad colour Use of unsuitable fruit; over-heating, failing to blanch (vegetables).

Bad flavour Poor variety; over cooking; under-ripe or stale fruit.

Squashed fruit   Much over-heating; too tight packing.

Rise in bottle   (Common) Loose packing; over-heating, rapid heating at the start; over-ripe fruit.

Sink in bottle   Loose packing; rapid heating; too heavy syrup. Pulping down indicates much overheating or for an excessive period.

Loss of colour   Apples turning brown caused by action of enzymes which should have been destroyed by placing the prepared apples in a lemon or acid solution at the beginning.

Air Bubbles   Especially in gooseberries; not easy to avoid but much improvement if the newly packed and filled bottles are jarred on the hand to cause the bubbles to rise to the top. (The packed 'bubbly' bottle is held in one hand and brought down upon the palm of the other hand fairly forcibly to dislodge the annoying bubbles which then leave the fruit and rise to the top.)

Hard skins   Sterilizing for too short a period, e.g. black currants, late plums, damsons. Cook before packing.

Mould   Not sufficiently sterilized; too rapid heating; seal not airtight.

Fermentation   Insufficient sterilization; over-ripe fruit.

INDEX

Uniform with this book

EASYMADE WINE & COUNTRY DRINKS

Mrs. Gennery-Taylor

Simplicity and economy are the keynotes of this book full of recipes for wines, beer, cider, children's drinks, and many more exciting beverages. All recipes are fully tested and proven. You can still make wine for less than 3p a bottle. No expensive equipment is required. All you need is a large saucepan or preserving pan, an earthenware or china bowl, and some bottles with corks. With these simple things, any competent housewife can amuse herself for hours, as well as providing her family with inexpensive, but often potent, alcoholic beverages.

This book is intended for the ordinary housewife or bachelor and is helpful to those who wish to make a few bottles for home consumption or for giving to friends.

ELLIOT RIGHT WAY BOOKS, KINGSWOOD, SURREY, U.K.